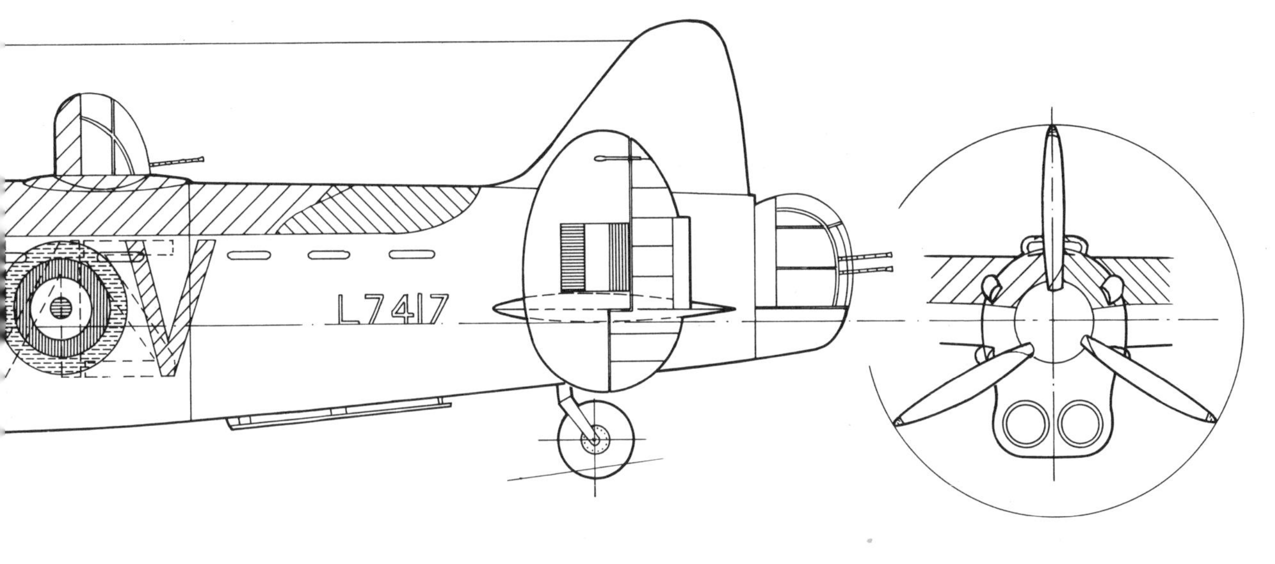

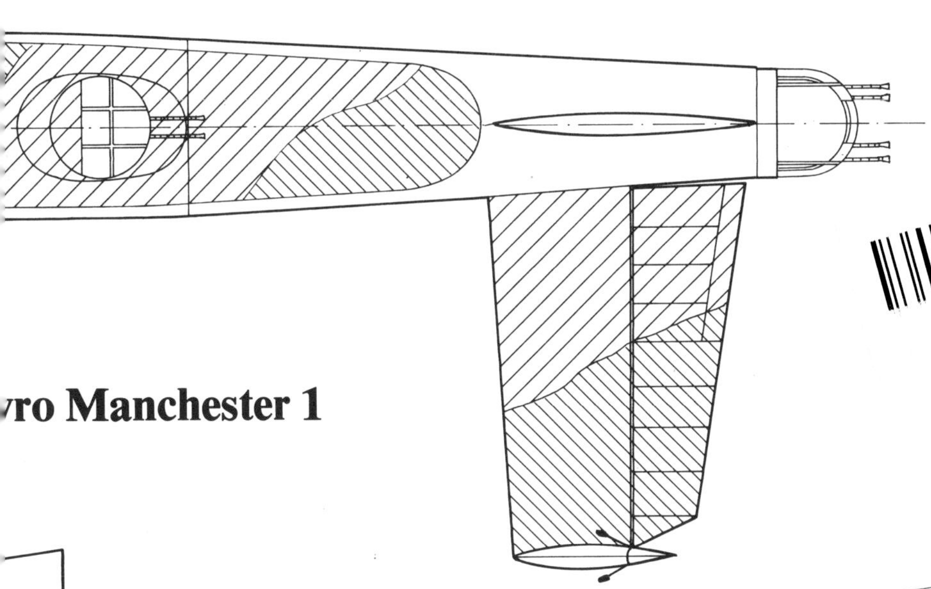

vro Manchester 1

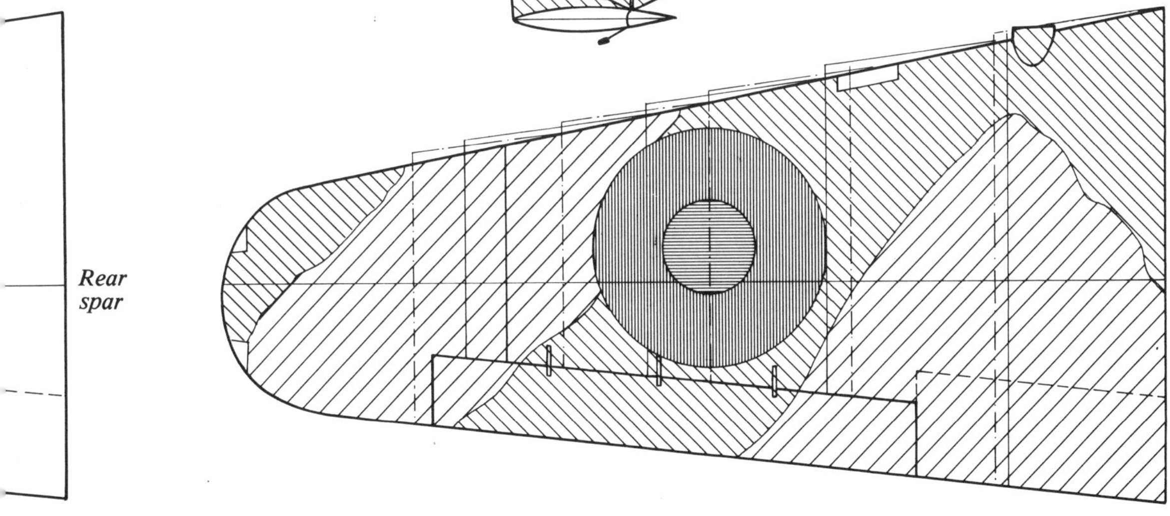

Rear spar

Lancaster

Classic Aircraft No.6
Their history and how to model them

Neville Franklin and Gerald Scarborough

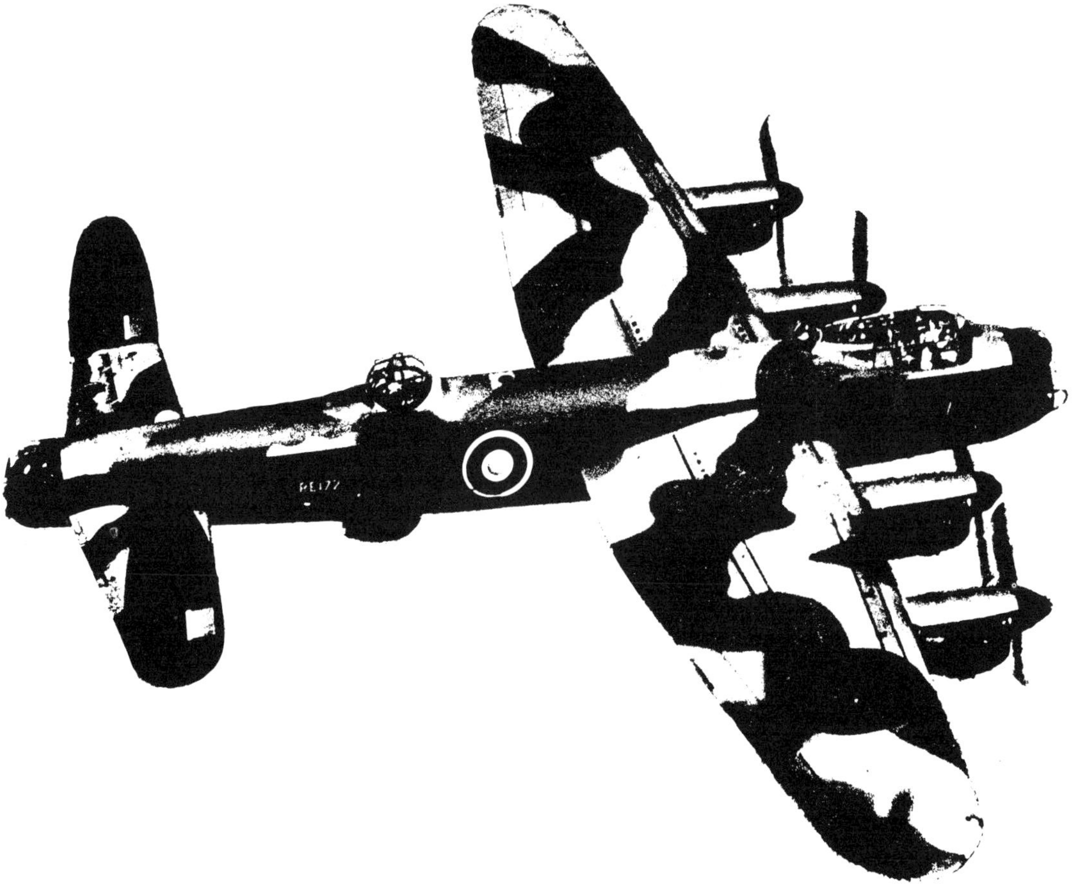

 Patrick Stephens, Cambridge

First published in 1979

British Library Cataloguing in Publication Data

Franklin, Neville
 Avro Lancaster—(Classic aircraft; no. 6).
 1. Lancaster (Bombers)
 I. Title   II. Scarborough, Gerald   III. Series
 623.74'63   UG1242.B6

 ISBN 0 85059 344 1

Front Cover *The Battle of Britain Flight Lancaster in her
heyday (MoD).*

Photoset in 9 on 10pt English Times
by Manuset Limited, 8 Sun Street, Baldock.
Printed in Great Britain on 100 gsm Pedigree coated
cartridge and bound by The Garden City Press,
Letchworth, for the publishers, Patrick Stephens
Limited, Bar Hill, Cambridge, CB3 8EL.

Contents

Introduction

When we were asked to write this book, we thought it superfluous due to the amount of literature available on bombing, etc, in World War 2 but researches have proved that there are still many unknown facts to uncover and, surprisingly, some are still 'classified'!

Statistics can be a very dry subject, but we believe that a few figures relating to the war effort of the Lancaster will be of interest.

The total number manufactured was 7,377 and the peak production occurred in August 1944 when 293 aircraft were delivered, together with the usual percentage of spare components, the airframe cost being £19,159 without engines and equipment.

Lancasters delivered almost exactly two-thirds of the total tonnage of bombs dropped by the Royal Air Force from the beginning of 1942. The figure is 608,612 tons or enough to fill a goods train about 345 miles long. Averaging four tons per bomber, this means well over 150,000 sorties, consuming more than 228 million gallons of fuel. In addition to the bomb loads, Avro Lancasters also delivered 51,513,106 incendiary bombs.

At the end of the war the Lancasters heralded a new era in aerial transport when they dropped 6,684 tons of food to the Dutch people, so earning the affectionate title of 'The Flying Grocer'.

A fitting conclusion to wartime exploits was provided by the repatriation of 74,178 ex-prisoners of war who made their journey home in Avro Lancasters.

Let Marshal of the Royal Air Force, Sir Arthur Harris have the last word on this war-winning bomber:

'The Lancaster surpassed all other types of heavy bomber. Not only could it take heavier bomb loads, not only was it easier to handle, not only were there fewer accidents with this than with other types throughout the war, the casualty rate of Lancasters was also considerably below other types. I used the Lancaster alone for those attacks which involved the deepest penetration into Germany and were, consequently, the most dangerous'.

The Lancaster was, without doubt, a most versatile aircraft, being converted directly into the Lancastrian transport and having the York utility transport developed from it, not to mention the many experimental variations and engine test-beds, the latter so ably covered by our good friend Dave Birch.

Our sincere thanks go to the many friends who have helped with photographs and anecdotes and these we list below, with apologies to any we might have forgotten.

Airfix Products, J.B. Allen, Chris Ashworth, H. Bachelor, Bill Baker, Battle of Britain Memorial Flight, Coningsby, David Bennett, Roy Benwell, Dave Birch, Roy Bonser, Paul E. Branke, Jack Bruce (RAF Museum), John Burgess, John and Sam Cooper, Roy Cross, Mrs Diana Davis BAeS, Philippe Denis, Dave Elvidge, B. Faux, Sid Finn, Dave Fletcher, Jerome Geeson, Brian Goulding, Peter Green, Bob Hambidge, Keith Hayward, Michael Hodgson, Harry Holmes BAeS, George Hopp, Graham Johnson, Ray Keightley, Peter Kirk, Neville Lockwood, Robert Löfberg, Peter Lord, Ian Macdonald, Norm Malayney, Greg Marshall, Geoffrey Moulds, Novo Toys Ltd, Bjorn Olsen, Luigi Passarrotto, S. Podsiadly, Dick Richardson (Strathallan), Brian Robinson, Rolls-Royce (Derby and Bristol), RAF Scampton, Revell (GB) Ltd, Rose Forgrove Ltd, Bill Rust, H.W. Sidwell, Skinners, Peter Studdart (Leicester Museum), Gordon Sutcliffe, John Tasker, Patrick Tilley (Blitz Publications), Alan Todd, John Walls, Chas Waterfall and long-suffering typists Jennifer M. Draper and Jane Scarborough.

Chapter One

Early developments

In 1936, the year Civil War broke out in Spain and introduced the world to tactical and strategic bombing as we know it today, eight of the front line bomber squadrons of the Royal Air Force were equipped with Handley Page Heyford 'express night bombers', three still had Vickers Virginias and one, 38 Squadron, was just re-equipping with Fairey Hendon Night Bombers, a monoplane spanning just over 100 feet, but still with a fixed undercarriage.

The US Army Air Corps, mainly equipped with Martin and Douglas twin-engined all-metal bombers, had flown their Boeing 299 (later XB-17) four motor bomber prototype on July 28 1935 although powered only, at that time, by four 750 hp Hornet radial engines but production versions, delivered between January and August of 1937, were powered by 930 hp Cyclone engines. The Luftwaffe had officially come into being in March 1935 and was already flying, in 'civil airliner' disguise, early models of Dornier Do 17, Heinkel He 111 and Junkers Ju 88, three bombers which, in successively modified versions, soldiered on through World War 2, whilst France, Japan and Russia boasted a motley collection of antique bombing planes, with no thoughts of heavier replacements.

Stalwart heavy bomber of the early days of World War 2, the Armstrong Whitworth Whitley first flew on March 17 1936, and the Wellington prototype had just flown when specification P13/36, dated September 8, was issued in November. This called for a twin-engined medium bomber weighing 20 tons (22.5 tonnes) to cruise at 275 mph at 15,000 ft on two-thirds maximum power carrying 3,000 lb bombs for 2,000 miles and with a maxi-mum bomb load of 8,000 lb, armour and power operated turrets in the nose and tail. The usual dimensions were specified, centre-section spar and longest fuselage section limited to 35 feet, any other section of wing or fuselage to 22 feet and all other components to 21 feet. It was also hoped that the aircraft could be used as a dive bomber, for torpedo dropping, as a troop carrier and with at least one parachute hatch in the floor for supply dropping, and all this on the power of two Rolls-Royce Vulture engines which were promised to give nearly 1,700 hp each!

Three companies submitted tenders, Avro, Handley Page and Hawker but, in the event, only the Avro proposal was constructed to the basic requirements of P13/36. Hawker's proposal was drafted by Sidney Camm and was submitted on January 1 1937 as a mid-wing monoplane with twin fins and rudder and this layout was also selected by George Volkert of Handley Page with his HP 56 and Roy Chadwick with his Avro Type 679 Manchester.

Handley Page already had their Heyford successor, the high-wing monoplane Harrow in production and Volkert, who admired the Douglas DC-2 airliner, had proposed the HP 55 with a Harrow type fuselage and tail, mounted on the low centre-section and swept outer wings of the American transport. Their submission to P13/36 was basically an enlarged version of this HP 55.

It is strange to note that, besides leading eventually to the war-winning Halifax and Lancaster heavy bombers, it also caused both their manufacturers to change completely their methods of construction. Previously, their aircraft, Heyford, Harrow and Avro's only

Armstrong Whitworth Whitley prototype K4586.

Above *A Vulture engine installed in a Manchester, with lifting jib erected.*

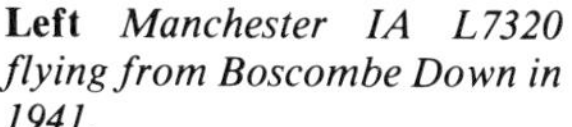

Left *Manchester IA L7320 flying from Boscombe Down in 1941.*

Left *The remains of Manchester L7300, EM-F of No 207 Squadron, Waddington, being salvaged by 58 MU.*

Right *Manchester prototype L7246 in August 1939.*

Right *Handley Page Harrow K6967 at Marham.*

production warplane, the long-lived Anson, which had first flown on March 24 1935, had fabric-covered steel tubular fuselages, whilst the new breed of bomber was of all-metal stressed skin construction like their American and German counterparts—and the Whitley—whilst the Wellington with its geodetic construction kept its fabric covering to the end.

Well, as can be seen, all the hopes of the P13/36 specification rested on the ostensibly powerful Rolls-Royce Vulture engine, and this was to prove their downfall. Rushed into production without sufficient development testing, the Vulture was a 24-cylinder poppet valve, liquid-cooled engine, with four banks of six cylinders in 'X' formation. Developed along with the smaller 12-cylinder Peregrine from the well-tried Kestrel, all three engines had a bore and stroke of 5 inches and $5\frac{1}{2}$ inches respectively, giving the Vulture a capacity of 42.48 litres. The four banks of cylinders were fitted to a common crankcase, and all was staked on the efficiency of its lubrication system and the bearings for its highly stressed single crankshaft. The piston, cylinder and valve-gear assemblies followed normal Rolls-Royce practice, four valves being fitted to each cylinder, operated by overhead camshafts, whilst ignition was effected by two independent screened magnetos. An SU down-draught carburettor was fitted and the air-fuel mixture delivered by a two-speed

supercharger to two main trunk pipes, each feeding two cylinder banks. Starting was by electric power using a ground supply, and the engine drove three-blade, fully feathering, constant-speed Rotol airscrews of 16 feet diameter. Power output was 1,845 hp at 3,000 rpm at an altitude of 5,000 ft with supercharger in low gear, whilst in high gear, 1,710 hp was developed at 15,000 ft.

Fortunately, perhaps, for Handley Page, sufficient Vulture engines were not available and, in 1937, the HP 56 was abandoned in favour of the HP 57 fitted with four Rolls-Royce Merlins and later known as the Halifax, although various alternative engines—two Sabres or Hercules, or four smaller engines, Taurus, Pegasus, Kestrel and Dagger were investigated. Similarly, a Manchester was delivered to Napiers for the fitting of two Sabres but the scheme was dropped and, with wings removed, it became an engine test stand. Two 2,520 hp Bristol Centaurus radial engines were actually fitted to another but this was not flown due to the advance made with the more effective Manchester III. (The Sabre and Centaurus Manchesters were to have been Mk IIs.) This was a standard Manchester fitted, after a conference between Ernest Hines and Roy Dobson, and later discussions with Air Chief Marshal Wilfrid Freeman (Air Member Development and Production), Air Marshal Tedder, both of whom had just flown in the second Manchester, and Major

A Vulture engine (Rolls-Royce Ltd).

G.P. Bulman (Director of Engine Production), with four Rolls-Royce Merlins.

The Vulture had first flown in the Henley prototype, K5115, which Hawker Aircraft had been asked to modify early in 1939. Within months it was sent to Hucknall, the Rolls-Royce test and development airfield. Unfortunately, the new engine was found to be insufficiently developed and another Henley, L3302, was similarly modified in 1940.

Despite test flying in the two Henleys and a Hawker Tornado, the Vulture suffered coolant circulation problems and then developed big-end failure due to a defect in the oil circulation system.

The first Manchester, L7246, with a wing span of 80 feet 2 inches and two small fins and rudder mounted at the ends of a 28 foot span tailplane and without any turrets, made its maiden flight at Ringway on July 25

1939 piloted by Captain H.A. Brown, Avro's chief test pilot. Early trials showed longitudinal instability and this was overcome by increasing the span by 9 feet 11 inches to 90 feet 1 inch. It also proved to be underpowered, a fact which had always worried Avro's design team.

Transferred to the Aircraft and Armament Experimental Establishment, Boscombe Down for service trials on its ninth flight on November 28, a third fin was added to improve directional stability but a forced landing in a cabbage field on December 12 ended the trials and the superficially damaged aircraft was dismantled and taken to Newton Heath for repair. The second prototype, L7247, fitted with a smaller central fin, had armament installed and first flew on May 26 1940. Two .303 Brownings were fitted in Frazer Nash nose, tail and FN 21A ventral turrets, but the latter was soon replaced by a Botha-type FN 7 dorsal turret, and a more rounded broad chord fin replaced the earlier crude central unit.

Two hundred Manchesters had been ordered earlier, straight off the drawing board and production commenced in July 1939. The carrying of torpedoes was deleted, as was the dive-bombing capability, but the idea of catapult launching was not given up until the first prototype, rebuilt, had visited Farnborough and actually been hurled in the air at a weight of 37,000 lb, three times the weight of the Heyford previously tested!

The first production aircraft, L7276, was delivered on August 5 1940 to Boscombe Down for trials, to be joined on October 25 by L7277, delayed by shortage of certain components, for service acceptance trials. The third Manchester was delivered to 27 MU, Shawbury, the same month, earmarked for No 207 Squadron reformed at Waddington on November 1. It arrived at its new home to join L7279 which had come via 6 MU at

Below *A side view drawing of EM-A.*

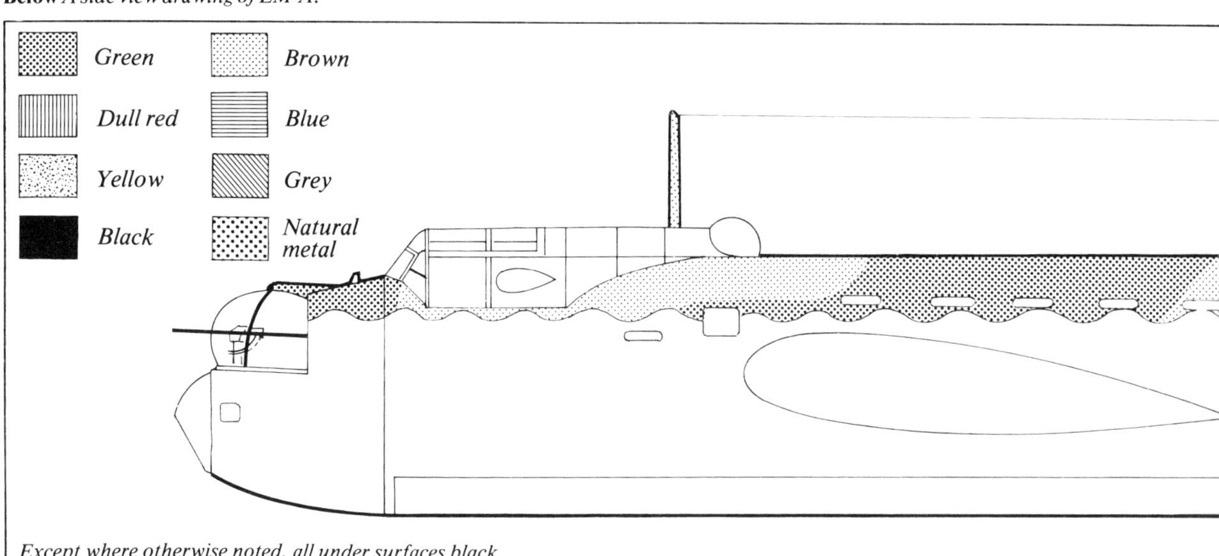

Except where otherwise noted, all under surfaces black.

Above *The fifth production Manchester, L7280, being erected at Woodford.*

Above *Vulture II Henley test-bed K5115* (Rolls Royce Ltd).

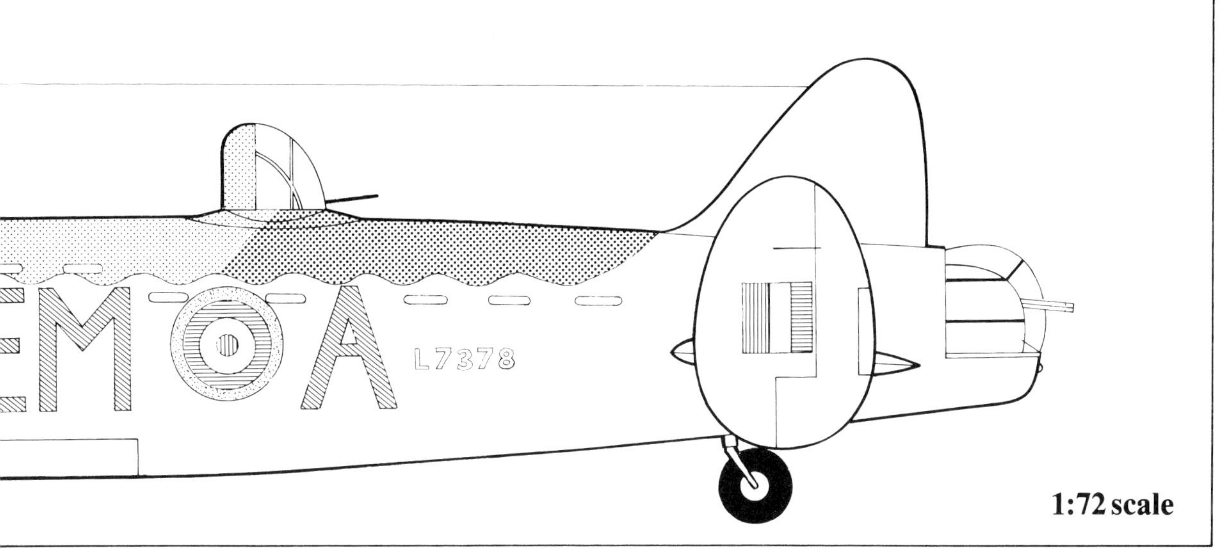

Brize Norton and the two aircraft were extensively flown to complete 500 flying hours with Rolls-Royce engineers supervising Vulture maintenance. Twenty-five production Manchesters had been completed by the end of 1940 but many were not serviceable, 207 Squadron struggling to keep four aircraft flying. Just after a visit by Their Majesties, King George VI and Queen Elizabeth, in January, the squadron was declared operational.

The first operation was on February 24 when six Manchesters bombed Brest, all returning although one crash landed back at Waddington due to failure of its hydraulics. This fault, affecting the mechanism of the undercarriage, caused further hold-ups and it was some weeks before the difficulties were overcome. Meantime, on March 5, the existence of the still secret Manchester was revealed to the public although no details were given.

New squadrons were being formed but the Vulture was not delivering sufficient power for safe operation. Engine failures were prevalent and, on April 13, after 15 raids, a general grounding was enforced with a further grounding on June 30 for engine checks and modifications. It is ironic that a Manchester, L7295, allocated to Rolls-Royce at Hucknall for engine development, crashed in flames at Ternhill on May 26 killing the test pilot, Reg Curlew. Soon after this it was decided to abandon production of the Vulture and to concentrate on the Merlin for bomber use.

Later production Manchesters had two larger fins mounted at the ends of a 33 foot span tailplane, deleting the centre fin. Many of the earlier ones were converted to Mk IAs by A.V. Roe and also Rollason Aviation at Tollerton near Nottingham. A.V. Roe produced 156 and Metropolitan Vickers completed 43 from a contract for 100 placed in 1939. These served with 13 squadrons and many training units until October/November 1943 when the remaining aircraft were struck off charge, although many soldiered on as training airframes with Lancaster squadrons and conversion units.

As already recorded, production aircraft spanned 90 feet 1 inch. They were 68 feet 10 inches long overall and 20 feet in height. Wing area was 1,131 square feet, the fuselage was 5 feet 9 inches wide and 8 feet 2 inches deep; the bomb bay was 33 feet long and main wheels of 5 feet 6 inches diameter. It carried a crew of six or seven, depending on the type of operation, and over five tons of bombs.

The Manchester was designed to be made in a number of sections to facilitate production, transport, maintenance and repair. The structure throughout had a skin of aluminium alloy sheet, flush riveting being employed to give a smooth external surface. The wing was of two-spar construction, each spar consisting of top and bottom extruded beams bolted to a single web plate. The ribs were aluminium alloy pressings, flanged and swaged for stiffness. The construction of the tailplane followed that of the wing.

The fuselage, in five parts, was built up of transverse formers and continuous longitudinal stringers. The roof of the bomb compartment formed the main cabin floor and two large, full-length doors were operated hydraulically by four rams—hence they always opened on the ground as the fluid leaked past the jack seals. The powerful hydraulic system (a new feature in those days) also operated the Dowty undercarriage, split trailing edge flaps, radiator and air intake shutters.

Unlike other heavy bombers, a canopy was fitted over the pilot's cockpit, enabling a clear view to be obtained in all directions including aft. The fighting controller's position was also situated inside this canopy, immediately aft of the pilot's seat and he too enjoyed an excellent view in every direction. Just aft of this position was the navigator's station with a table and adequate stowage space for charts, etc, and in the roof of the cabin was an astro-dome. The wireless operator's station was at the rear end of the navigator's table, just forward of the front spar. At this point, an armour-plated bulkhead was fitted across the centre-section portion of the fuselage, this being designed to open up on each side of the centre line for access purposes. Additional armour plating was provided at the back of the pilot's seat and behind his head, and special bullet-proof glass was used to give further protection to the fire controller. Certain other vulnerable parts of the aircraft's structure, including the turrets, were armour plated.

In the fuselage, near the mid-upper turret position, space was provided for the stowage of flares, emergency rations, etc. The ammunition boxes were also located in this part of the fuselage, ammunition being supplied from them to the tail turret by means of tracks. There was a walk-way from the tail turret forward to the other crew stations and the main entrance door to the fuselage was situated on the starboard side just forward of the tailplane. Escape hatches were provided, at suitable points, for all the crew.

The bomb aimer's station was in the nose below the front turret and forward of the pilot's cockpit. A dinghy, carried in the trailing edge portion of the centre section of the port wing, was automatically released in the event of a crash landing, but could also be released by hand. Fuel, 1,160 gallons of it, was carried in self-sealing tanks in the wings.

With a maximum speed of 265 mph at 17,000 feet, best cruising speed 185 mph at 15,000 feet, and service ceiling of 19,200 feet (with two engines working properly!), this was not a war-winning aircraft. Of the 200 actually built, over 30 per cent (ie, 63) were lost on operations and a similar percentage (59) written off in accidents during training or for technical reasons. But 1,269 sorties were flown, equally by day and night, 1,826 tons of high explosive plus incendiaries and sea-mines were dropped during just five months in 1941.

However, one must realise that it replaced the popular but ineffective Hampden in many squadrons and it did lead to the Manchester III, later re-named the Lancaster.

Chapter Two

The Lanc is blooded

With the virtual scrapping of Vulture development, a standard Manchester airframe was selected from the production line around mid-1940—the exact date is impossible to pin-point due to the surprising lack of documentation—and fitted with four Merlin engines. With the availability of two sets of longer spar extrusions already ordered for a proposed Manchester span increase, it was also fitted with wings of 12 feet additional span. The Merlin power plant had been developed by Rolls-Royce at Hucknall for installation in the Beaufighter II and could be fitted unchanged to new nacelles on the extended outer mainplanes, little modification to the cowlings being required to fit it to the existing Vulture nacelles.

Thus the Avro 683 Lancaster was born, BT308 the first prototype, still with a triple-fin tail unit. It made its first flight on January 9 1941, about the time when the Manchester was entering squadron service. Intensive flight trials of this Lancaster at A&AEE Boscombe Down from February 28 proved it to be a success and BT308, now fitted with twin fins and a 33-foot span tailplane, was demonstrated to No 44 Squadron at Waddington on September 15 as this unit had been selected to receive the first production machines.

Meanwhile, the second prototype, DG595, fitted with Merlin XX engines of 1,280 hp and a stronger undercarriage to cope with its increased weight, flew on May 13. The success of this quickly-modified airframe, the high commonality with the Manchester, and its obvious potential, ended production of the Vulture-powered machines with L7526. The next batch of airframes off the line, already partially completed, were finished as Lancaster B Mk 1s, L7527 flying at Woodford on October 31 1941. This was allocated to Boscombe Down for trials and the next went to the Tele-communication Flying Unit at Hurn for the installation and testing of radio equipment. L7529 also went to Boscombe Down, whilst the next Lancaster was allocated to No 44 (Rhodesia) Squadron.

This unit had received its first three, L7537, L7538 and L7541, on Christmas Eve of 1941 and, by March 1942, 25 of the first batch had been delivered. The intensive working-up period made the squadron non-operational while pilots were converted, gunners practised in their turrets, armourers loaded and unloaded various combinations of stores and ground crews worked out their maintenance routine. Service manuals were not, of course, yet available but the general similarity to the Manchester enabled the first four Lancasters to lay mines in the Heligoland Bight on March 3 after several earlier ops had been scrubbed because of bad weather. Carrying four 'Vegetables' instead of the single one of the Hampden, the new aircraft's longer range enabled minefields to be laid in areas previously immune. The first bombs were dropped on Essen on March 10 by two Lancasters, whilst eight of the squadron were at Lossiemouth preparing for an attack on the *Tirpitz*, then at Trondheim.

An early production Lancaster at dispersal.

An unidentified Lancaster being made ready for its 11th sortie. The boxes are incendiary canisters (Photographic News Agencies Ltd).

The second squadron to be equipped with Lancs was No 97 (Straits Settlements) Squadron at Coningsby, this unit having moved from Waddington with its Manchesters in March 1941. Its first Lancasters arrived in January 1942 and it was mine-laying off the Friesian Islands by March 20.

Production was increasing, the Metropolitan-Vickers Manchester lines had changed over to the Lancaster and their first went to Avro's Woodford factory for final assembly on January 5. The Lancaster Aircraft Group's Yeadon shadow factory was visited by King George VI and Queen Elizabeth on March 20 when the King named R5498 'George' and the Queen named R5548 'Elizabeth'. These aircraft were subsequently delivered to No 44 and No 97 Squadrons respectively, but neither was to survive to the end of the year.

No 97 Squadron's Lancasters were taken off ops on March 26 when one was lost due to the structural failure of an outer wing. No 5 Group, in whose area all the Lancasters were operating, signalled, 'Lancaster aircraft to be inspected immediately for failure of flush rivets attaching the wing tip skin to rib attachment to mainplane and wrinkling of skin on the top surface. Aircraft defective are to be grounded until further

This unidentified Lancaster, coded JF-D, was used for demonstrating dismantling techniques—it is seen 'somewhere in Scotland'.

instructions. Aircraft not defective may be flown on practice flights only, with light load inboard tanks only. Remaining tanks to be empty'. Eight aircraft were found to be in need of rectification and were withdrawn.

Contemporary thoughts were that bombers could be used in daylight and, indeed, Stirlings had in 1941 proved that their three power-operated turrets gave good defence, so it is not surprising that the Lancaster should also have been used by day. The loss of merchant shipping and the build-up of the German submarine force were, in 1942, two of the worst problems facing the Allies. Coastal Command was much under strength so help from Bomber Command was sought despite protests that this was not their strategic aim. Hence, besides having Lancasters detached for sea patrols, attacks on submarine pens and 'gardening' (mining) sorties, many of the night raids were on shipyards and ports. This affected the planning behind the Augsburg raid on April 17, surely the most daring and costly attack of the war!

Twelve Lancasters, six from each of the squadrons equipped, and each carrying four 1,000-pounders with 11-second fuses, were to make the 1,250-mile round trip to bomb the submarine diesel shop of the Maschinen-fabrik Augsburg Nürnburg AG in southern Germany. The four 'Vics', led by Squadron Leader D.J. Nettleton, had practised low-flying in Scotland and their tactics were 20 years ahead of those then in use—and all the piloting and navigation was then manual! Low level pinpointing was used, radar aids not having been developed, and the timed attack over Lake Constance was also reminiscent of current off-set bombing. The formation was bounced by 30 Messerschmitt Bf 109s of JG 2, the Richthofen Geschwader, their over-shooting cannon shells crashing into buildings, blowing holes in walls and scattering cattle in the fields; thus only two of the 44 Squadron aircraft arrived at the target. Nettleton attacked, followed by Flying Officer Garwell whose Lanc was immediately hit and caught fire. Only five of the 12 aircraft were able to limp home protected by darkness, all badly damaged. However, eight aircraft had bombed the target with the main diesel shop suffering severe damage.

Nettleton was awarded the VC, his crew were all honoured. The RAF still acknowledges his magnificent effort by coding their last flying Lancaster KM-B, the same code as was carried that day in 1942.

It was to be six months before another daylight raid was made by Lancasters and then, on October 17, 94 set out, almost all the Lancaster force, from nine squadrons by then equipped, all in No 5 Group. Again a full-scale rehearsal was held, on October 1, and over 100 Lancasters with fighters making mock attacks, flew over England to the Wash and dropped their bombs on Wainfleet Range. Strict security was enforced, the target remaining unknown to crews until the day of the raid proper. Visitors to the bases had to remain on the premises until the bombers had departed. Coastal Command Whitleys patrolled the Channel to keep U-

Lancasters practising for a daylight sortie.

boats down and ensure that no patrol boats would be in a position to report the approaching armada. These precautions paid off, the squadrons forming up over Upper Heyford before setting course for Land's End, then sweeping out over the Bay of Biscay before turning in over occupied France, a ten-hour flight. The Lancasters met no fighters and only light flak on their 300-foot run-in to the Schneider works at Le Creusot, the French equivalent of Krupps. The formation opened out and climbed just before the target to avoid congestion. The attack commenced at dusk and bombs were seen to hit the target, over 100 tons of explosives and 40 tons of incendiaries being dropped from an average height of only 6,000 feet.

Only one Lancaster failed to return and two Arado seaplanes were shot down by an aircraft returning alone. When photographic reconnaissance reports were received, it was found that, whilst much damage had been done, the greater part of the arms factory was still standing! This was attributed to the lack of daylight training so, for another 18 months, the Lanc flew by night.

The early years of the war had produced very poor bombing results, indeed it sometimes proved very difficult or even impossible to identify the actual areas bombed from target photos taken. The introduction of 'Gee', early in 1942, was the first step towards improved accuracy. This navigation aid had been under development since 1940 at the Telecommunications Research Establishment and depended on pulsed signals received from three transmitters. From these, the aircraft's position could be plotted on a special lattice chart and, as will be seen, it was not subject to navigation inaccuracies occasioned by compass or speed errors, nor affected by variable winds. It was reckoned that successful jamming could be expected within six months, so its use was not envisaged until at least 200 bombers had been equipped. The only limitation of Gee was its range, dependent on the curvature of the Earth and the height of the aircraft receiving the signal, making the limit some 350-400 miles.

On February 20 1942, Air Marshal Arthur Harris became Bomber Command's new Commander-in-Chief and he took over 44 squadrons, 38 of them operational. But only 14 of the total were equipped with the new heavy bombers (Stirlings, Manchesters and Halifaxes), 30 still having the old heavy bombers, now referred to as 'medium bombers' (Whitleys, Hampdens and Wellingtons) with which the war began. By the beginning of 1943, seven more squadrons had been formed—about 200 more aircraft—but more important, with the introduction of the newer heavies, especially the Lancaster, Bomber Command's effectiveness in bomb carrying ability was increased by 70 per cent.

Of 211 aircraft which took off for the first Gee raid on Germany, 82 were so equipped and Essen was the target, as it was the next night. Both raids were a disappointment, the giant Krupps works escaping virtually untouched although the great Thyssen steel works in nearby Hamborn accidentally received a heavy attack! Two further raids on Essen in the same month also proved unsuccessful and Gee appeared to be ineffective or was not being used correctly. Its accuracy at maximum range was four to five miles, leaving the actual targets to be identified visually, a difficult task for a bomb-aimer dazzled by his own flares particularly when industrial haze and the brightness of the Moon

added to the problem. A hooded flare was required, this being introduced as the target indicator bomb.

The highest number of bombers ever used against a single target to this date had been 228 out of an average number of 350 available. Thus the idea of using 1,000 bombers was not only novel but, apparently, impossible. Backed by Churchill, Bomber Command planned Operation Millenium, using bombers from the Operational Training Units, and Cologne was attacked on May 30. Of the 1,046 aircraft used, 367 were from training units but, more important, 338 were heavy bombers including 75 Lancasters all carrying a 4,000-pound bomb and incendiaries. The Gee-equipped Wellingtons and Stirlings of No 1 and No 3 Groups dropped the first bombs at 17 minutes past midnight and the last Lancasters set off at 0225 hours. Over 900 aircraft made a successful attack, dropping about 2,100 tons. The total loss was 44 aircraft, only 3.9 per cent of the total force, much lower than normally expected. As Harris had forecast, the defences were swamped and 600 acres of Cologne were laid waste, even a German communiqué admitted 'great damage'.

In August 1942 the Pathfinders were formed, a separate force of experienced crews, to find and mark targets. Four squadrons, Nos 7 (Stirlings), 35 (Halifaxes), 83 (Lancasters) and 156 (Wellingtons) were initially allocated, one from each Bomber Group, with 109 Squadron carrying out experimental work on radio counter-measures and new radar aids. Commanded by Australian Group Captain Donald Bennett, it became No 8 (PFF) Group on January 8 1943 and eventually re-equipped with Lancasters and Mosquitos. Their first operation on August 18, in bad weather and just after the Germans had discovered Gee and had begun its jamming, was unsuccessful, the Flensburg submarine yard escaping on this occasion. Proficiency improved by the end of the war as experience was gained and new

A side elevation of the well-known R5689, VN-N of No 50 Squadron, Swinderby, August 1942.

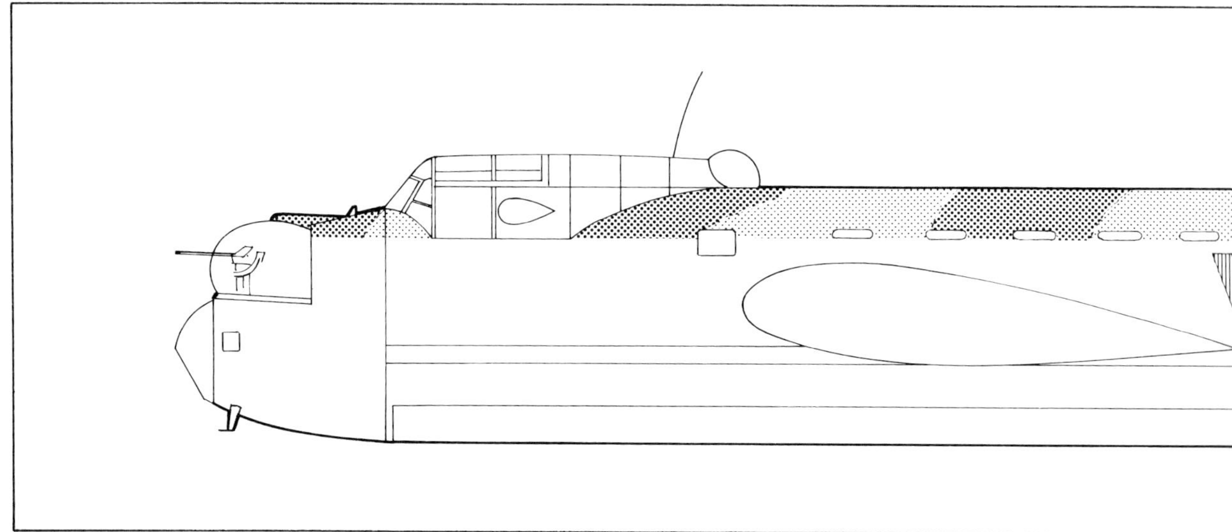

methods were developed, and the TI (Target Indicator) Bomb became available in October.

The Battle of the Ruhr opened successfully on March 5 1943 when 442 bombers using the newly-introduced bombing and navigation aid 'Oboe' ravaged Essen. Led by eight Oboe-equipped Mosquitos and 22 heavy bombers of the Pathfinder Force, Krupps' works, covering several acres in the heart of the city, received attention for the first time. In the next few months, Essen received five more visits, the last on July 25 when 700 aircraft took part, leaving the city and Krupps largely in ruins. Next to suffer in the Ruhr was Duisburg, home of heavy industry and an inland port, receiving over 5,000 tons of bombs in five raids.

Perhaps the greatest raid of them all, at least the one which gained the most publicity, and rightly so, achieving the greatest effect per aircraft lost, was the attack on the dams supplying the Ruhr valley with hydro-electric power. No 617 Squadron was formed especially for this attack which was planned and the special mine and aircraft developed, in less than three months from when the go-ahead was given on February 26 1943. Barnes Wallis had been working on large bombs since the war began in 1939.

At this time, the Royal Air Force's largest bomb was the 500-pounder, designed at the end of World War I and some had been in store since 1919! A 1,000-pounder had been proposed in 1926 but was vetoed by the Treasury; anyway how could you aim them?! A stick of small bombs had a better chance of hitting the target, hadn't it? It was not until the Luftwaffe was dropping sticks of bombs on our factories and houses that it was possible to see how ineffective they were—a stick of seven small bombs dropped on a factory had damaged only 24 out of 500 machines and only two were beyond repair!

By mid-May, the dams were expected to be at their highest level, hence the top priority given to the building of 20 special Lancasters and the Scampton steam-roller,

a cylindrical mine 50 inches in diameter and five feet long. Experimental drops of scale mines, of varying shapes, had earlier been made from a specially modified Wellington flown by Vickers test pilot, 'Mutt' Summers off Chesil Beach on the south coast. The first of the three test prototypes for the Lancaster B III Specials, ED765/G (the 'G' indicated that the aircraft must be guarded at all times due to secret equipment it contained), was delivered to Farnborough on April 8 1943. Tests of the full-size weapon were being made off Reculver in Kent, the second prototype, ED817/G joining in, flying from Manston on April 20, but it was not until the 29th that a successful drop was made, earlier models having broken up whilst skipping along the surface of the sea.

The new squadron, commanded by Wing Commander Guy Gibson, a veteran of three tours (157 ops), had been practising low flying much to the disgust of the locals. Initially the flying was by day with canopies fitted giving two-stage amber screening, later flying was at night. Earlier, a small disused dam high in the Welsh hills west of Leominster in Radnorshire (now Powys), 150 feet long and quite thick, had been breached by Barnes Wallis in experiments to determine the minimum amount of RDX explosive required. Now the Lake District thundered to the sound of Merlins, 617's Lancasters using the area for low flying practice but still not knowing why!

The first production-modified Lancaster, ED864/G, arrived at Scampton on April 18, the twentieth being delivered on May 13. The crews viewed their new mount with apprehension; it appeared to them as a designer's nightmare! The bomb doors had gone, two V-shaped support brackets were fitted with pivots and a V-belt drive to the starboard one, two fairing doors were fitted at the front but the rear of the bomb bay was just faired in. The mid-upper turret was removed to save weight, the opening being faired flush; and two spotlights were fitted and aligned to intersect exactly 60 feet below the

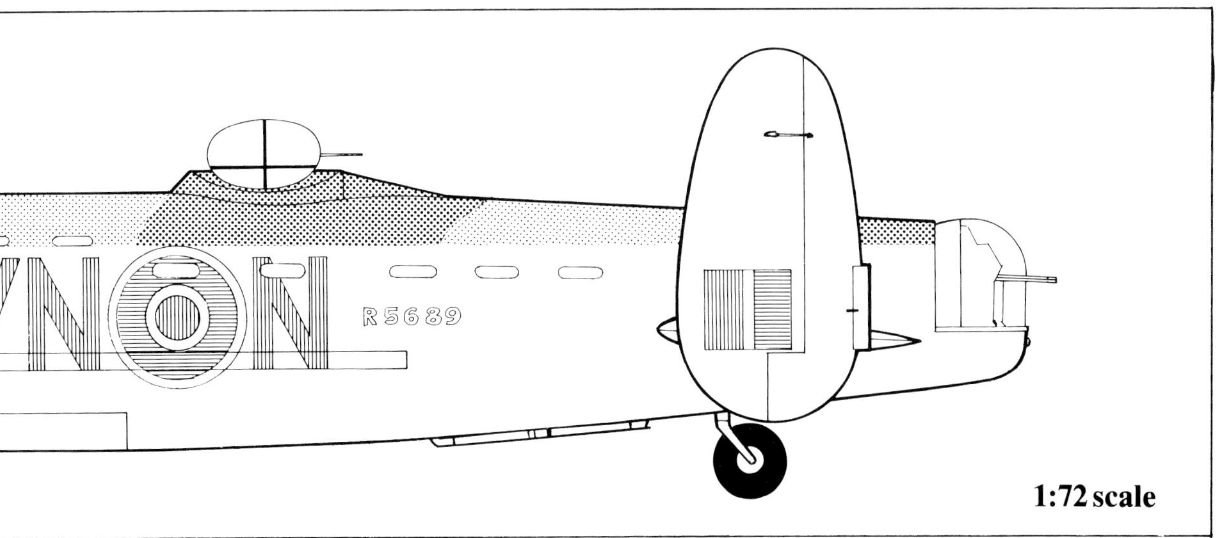

Lancaster and slightly to starboard so that the crew navigator could check the accuracy of their height with this 'Spotlight Altimeter Calibrator'.

Originally a Ford V8 engine was to be fitted in the fuselage to spin the store at 500 rpm before release, but this proved too heavy. With the elimination of the 33-foot long bomb doors, it was found possible to bolt a VSG hydraulic motor to the cockpit floor using the surplus power made available. The standard bomb-sight proved useless and this produced another problem which was eventually solved very simply. It was discovered that the two most important dams, both masonry types, had two control towers 600 feet apart. The drop was made a quarter of a mile from the dam to allow the mine to skip along the surface over the anti-torpedo nets, slow down before reaching the wall and drop down into the water. It was a simple geometrical problem to put two nails and a sight on a piece of plywood. This proved easy to use and effective!

In the short period from its formation, the experienced crews of 617 Squadron, for Gibson had been given the pick of No 5 Group and had chosen those nearing the end of a tour to spare upsetting their squadrons too much, had flown 2,000 hours on training flights and dropped some 2,500 practice bombs. One of the 20 special Lancasters was damaged a few days before the raid when Squadron Leader Maudsley dropped a mine too low and water damaged the underside of the aircraft, hence only 19 aircraft were ready to go on May 16 when the water level in the German dams was just over one metre from its maximum.

Last of the three experimental prototypes, ED825/G, was hastily flown to Scampton from Boscombe Down on that busy Sunday to act as a spare aircraft and a recent report indicates that American Flight Lieutenant Joe McArthur took this to the Sorpe Dam when his aircraft ED923/G became unserviceable as he taxied out.

It was not until Saturday May 15 that most of the crews learned the identity of their targets. Models of the three dams to be attacked, Moehne, Eder and Sorpe, had been carefully made for planning the final attack—a dive from 2,000 feet to a precise 60 feet *and* an exact 232 mph! The Moehne Dam, 40 metres high, held back 140 million tons of water, the Eder Dam 60 miles away to the south-east and of similar height held 202 million tons, whilst the earth dams of Ennepe, Sorpe, Uster and Schwelme of smaller capacity, had a lower priority.

The nineteen Lancasters, with their cylindrical mines in place, loaded by lifting them by the tail and lowering the aircraft on to the roller, were split into three formations, nine aircraft in three waves taking off at ten-minute intervals and led by Guy Gibson, followed by five aircraft in loose formation intended to be led by

'Details from A.V. Roe drawing No Z2353 (April 1 1943)—diagram of loading (Type 464 provisioning)—Most Secret'.

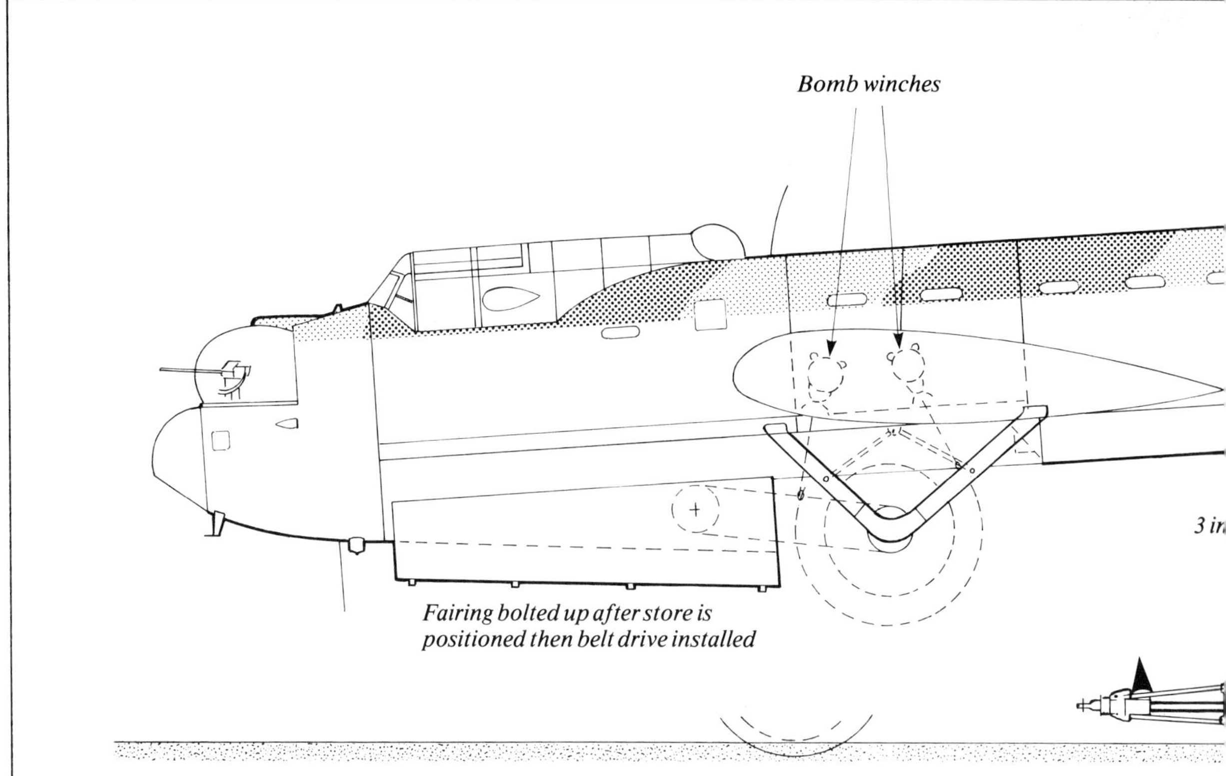

Joe McCarthy, and the five reserve aircraft leaving two hours later. The second wave left first as their northern route was longer, but their leader's aircraft had to be changed, perhaps luckily for him as, of the others, only two returned, Flight Lieutenant Munro with radio failure and Pilot Officer Rice after hitting the Zuyder Zee with his spotlight altimeter not working and losing his mine, whilst the other two Lancs were never seen again.

Gibson's formation, taking off from 2130 hours, with nearly five tons of bombs (the weapon weighed 9,250 lb and housed 6,600 lb of RDX explosive) and over five tons of petrol, and flying at heights as low as 40 feet, lost only one aircraft which, off course, disappeared. Vicious flak was received and searchlights were troublesome but successfully dealt with by vigilant nose and tail gunners. With eight Lancs circuiting round the Moehne lake, Gibson dropped the first mine at 20 minutes after midnight that Monday morning and, half an hour later, after the fifth attack and the loss of another aircraft, Hutchison, Gibson's wireless operator, was signalling 'Nigger' in morse back to base. The dam had been breached and a wall of water 25 feet high rolled down the valley.

Gathering the rest of the formation, Gibson headed for the Eder Dam, a much more difficult target to attack, with fog filling the valley and 1,000-foot ridges to clear on the run in. Flight Lieutenant Dave Shannon attacked first but after five unsuccessful runs withdrew

to study the problem. Squadron Leader Maudsley made the next run, dropping his mine at the third attempt but too late as it hit the top of the parapet and the Lancaster disappeared in a blinding flash. Then Shannon tried again, placing his mine perfectly on his second run. Pilot Officer Knight was the last to attack with the last mine and dropped this successfully at his third attempt. Watching anxiously, they saw huge chunks of masonry flying into the air and the water gushed out as in a tidal wave.

Two mines were successfully dropped on the earth dam at Sorpe and one at Ennerpe, all moving loads of earth but not effectively.

The Ruhr, which had been bombed regularly since the introduction of Gee, was now flooded with 330 million tons of water. Fifty miles from the dams factories collapsed, railways and bridges disappeared, as did a large airfield at Fritzlar, thousands were made homeless, hundreds were drowned, and the shortage of water, both for domestic and industrial use, was the worst problem of all, as Bomber Command had hoped.

The cost: eight Lancasters did not return, only two of their crews being saved. Guy Gibson received the VC and 32 other decorations were awarded.

No information on the Lancaster's special modifications, or the weapon so successfully developed by Barnes Wallis, was released until the end of 1962—but the Germans had found an intact mine in one of the drained reservoirs the next morning!

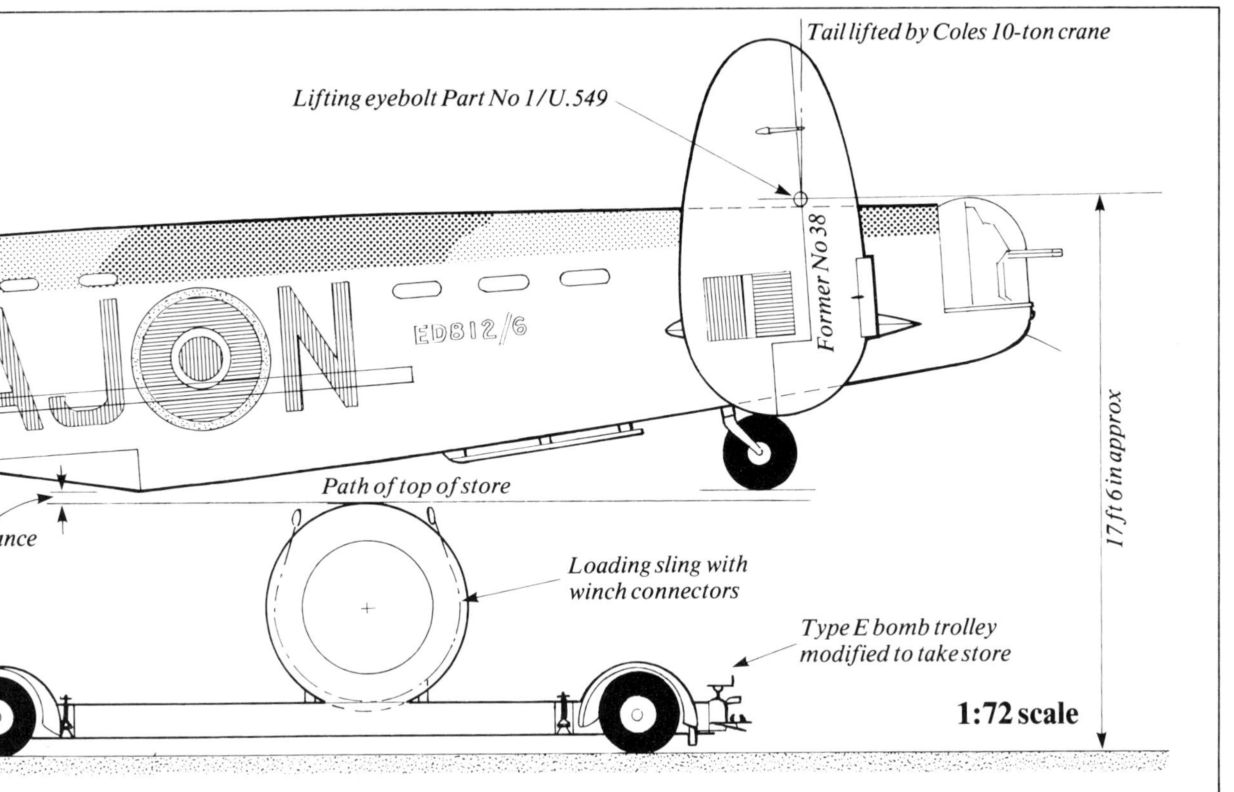

The Lancasters remaining were converted back to standard, but 617 Squadron, the dams raid commemorated for all time in its crest, soldiered on from Coningsby maintaining its quickly-gained reputation as an élite unit and carrying on its tradition today as a Vulcan squadron.

Dusseldorf was attacked twice, the second raid on June 11-12 by 693 aircraft causing severe damage. Ninety per cent of Wuppertal-Barmen was destroyed on May 29-30 in an attack by 534 bombers, 33 of which did not return, mainly lost to radar-equipped night fighters—the contest between scientists was hotting up!

A minor but innovatory raid by a force of 54 Lancasters led by four H_2S equipped pathfinders, took place on June 20. Earlier that month, a PI (Photo Interpreter) at Medmenham had been studying photographs of a new radar with a parabolic dish 20 feet in diameter. He concluded that the supporting metal framework was reminiscent of the construction of the early Zeppelins, so he dug out the most up-to-date coverage of the former airship workshop at Friedrichshafen on the shores of Lake Constance which, it was known, was engaged on secret war work. There he identified stacks of components resembling the trellis framework and, in less than a week, No 5 Group Lancs had been briefed to attack. A master bomber directed the raid and over half the factory which was producing radar equipment for the German night fighter force, and the wind tunnel, together with several repair shops and half the foundry, were destroyed. The bombers had reached their target unmolested, but the night fighters were on the alert awaiting their return—however, the force continued southwards to land in North Africa! La Spezia in Northern Italy was attacked on the homeward journey, again without loss although one 44 Squadron Lancaster was left behind in North Africa due to unserviceability, highlighting the principal disadvantage of shuttle bombing. Turin was attacked on July 12, routing well out over the Bay of Biscay and across southern France. This was expected to be a low risk raid but 44 Squadron lost Wing Commander J.D. Nettleton VC in ED331 which was believed to have strayed over the Brest Peninsula on its way home and been shot down. A second shuttle raid was made on July 16 when a small force attacked a power station near Reggio in Italy, going on to land at Blida. Bad weather in England delayed their return trip and an attack on Leghorn for a week, giving time to load the Lancasters full of lemons, grapes and other fruit plus some wine. Shortly after 44 Squadron's Lancs landed back at Dunholme Lodge, the Station Commandant, the Squadron Commander, their WAAF drivers, ground and air crews could be seen standing around the dispersals eating grapes, and some local pubs ended up with stocks of lemons!

The night before the last raid on Essen, Harris opened the Battle of Hamburg. 791 bombers attacked on July 25 in the first of four great raids, using 'window', strips of metallised paper for blanking out the screens of the German's defensive radar. The ancient town was near the coast and easily identifiable on the screens of the new H_2S plan position indicators first used by the Pathfinder Force. The first attack of Operation Gomorrah ('Sodom' was Essen) included a high proportion of incendiaries to saturate the fire services. 740 bombers dropped 2,396 tons of bombs between 0100 and 0330 hours, only 12 not returning, 'window' was proving its value in interfering with radar controlled searchlights and flak. German GCI fighter control stations were thrown into confusion and wireless listening stations in England heard night fighters being told to seek their own targets. 'Window' had been available for a long time but neither side had dared to use it for fear of its effect when used by their opponents! Home defences in the United Kingdom were now deemed so strong that reprisal raids were no longer feared, but the saving of friendly bombers was of great importance.

Small daylight raids on Hamburg were made by USAAF bombers on the same day as the RAF's first raid on that city on the 26th, giving the defences, fire and rescue service no respite. 739 bombers again attacked in good weather on the night of July 27-28, dropping over 2,400 tons of bombs.

German reports spoke of the resultant firestorm and this was added to the next night when 2,382 tons were dropped by another 726 bombers. The whole of Hamburg was on fire, water, gas and electricity supplies all failed, the city being knocked out as even the undamaged areas had to stop work due to the lack of services.

The last raid on Hamburg, made by Lancasters alone due to the bad weather and cloud expected up to 20,000 feet, was made on the night of August 2-3. This was a lighter raid but the interval had allowed some reorganisation of the night fighter defences, a running commentary on the progress of the bomber stream being broadcast to the waiting night fighters on standing patrol. Thirty bombers failed to return but more than 6,000 acres of Hamburg smouldered in ruins, although its recovery was quicker than could have been expected.

Despite the short nights, August was a busy month. Mannheim was the target on August 9 with Nürnburg the next night, whilst Milan was attacked on the 12th, 14th and 15th in quick succession.

A report received from Oslo early in the war spoke of secret weapons being developed by the Germans, pilotless bombers and long range rockets. This had been treated with scepticism but some details in the report proved correct and a committee was formed on April 12 1943 to review reports received in England and America and the threats of secret weapons put out in Nazi propaganda broadcasts. Mention was made of Swinemünde and Peenemünde. The latter was known to be a research centre suspected of rocket research. Special photographic sorties were made to the area in April and June and two large, torpedo-shaped objects, some 40 feet long were detected, so a bombing attack was ordered.

Due to the distance involved, it was not possible to schedule a raid before the longer nights of mid-August and the date was fixed for August 17-18. The target was scattered, the purposes of the various buildings were not known, and the long flight would give enemy fighters time to get in to position for the return journey unless some new tactics were evolved. Nearly 600 bombers were laid on for the attack and a deception was planned. A mere 20 Mosquitos were to make a feint attack on Berlin, dropping a multitude of flares and creating the impression—successfully as it turned out—that they were over the major target. Over 200 night fighters searched the skies above Berlin in vain and received the full force of the city's flak!

Three aiming points were marked and Group Captain J.H. Searby of No 83 Squadron was master bomber. The attack was timed to start at 0200 hours, by which time the first enemy fighters, Messerchmitt Bf 110s of II/NJG 1, were on their way from Berlin. The Moon was bright but there was a good deal of cloud, and a smoke screen was laid. Nearly 2,000 tons of bombs were dropped and the attack was successful, work on the V-2 rocket being held up for two months by loss of vital parts, drawings, designers and engineers. The cost was high, 40 bombers, including 17 Lancasters, failed to return.

'Bomber' Harris had long wished to attack Berlin, and Winston Churchill was in full agreement, but more important industrial targets had been rated of higher priority. With the Ruhr still staggering from its heavy blows, and other cities smouldering, Berlin was to receive three raids on August 23 and 31 and September 3, but night fighters were waiting and the Halifaxes and Stirlings suffered most. Thus the last raid was an all-Lancaster effort, 20 being lost, some improvement on the 100-odd missing from the first two raids.

Berlin covered a big area and it was not to suffer like Hamburg, but much damage was done, although it would take many more raids to make any great impression. Sixteen major raids were made in this period, some very heavy and the last being on March 24-25 1944. Good weather was never found, Pathfinders frequently 'skymarking' the target above cloud. Strangely, the western half of the city received the greater proportion of the damage, this being heaviest in the neighbourhood of the Tiergarten.

The most effective raid was that of February 15-16 1944 when, in just 39 minutes, 806 bombers dropped 2,642 tons of bombs through thick cloud, losing 42 of their number. The attack was noted for its precision, despite the city never being seen and the last arrivals reported a column of smoke rising 30,000 feet. Hits were made that night on Siemens and Halske, electrical manufacturers, 142 other factories, two gas works, a power station, five tramway depots and the broadcasting station.

Bomber Command lost 492 aircraft in the 16 major raids on Berlin, 5.4 per cent of those despatched, and destroyed 2,180 acres—over four square miles! Factories damaged included the Daimler-Benz aero-engine works, Lorenz, two principal AEG factories and Siemens. One can only ponder on Göring's promise, 'No enemy plane will fly over the Reich territory', which appeared on the nose of R5868, the famed 'S' for Sugar, now in the RAF Museum.

During the winter of 1943-44, many more targets were hit, mainly industrial, and not all successfully. The attack on the Schweinfurt ball-bearing factory on February 24-25 by 734 aircraft, about 550 of which were Lancasters, was one of the least successful, only 22 of the bombers finding the target whilst 33 were lost. This was part of the so-called 'Big Week', a joint RAF/USAAF attack on the German aircraft industry when 16,500 tons of bombs were dropped in six days and nights, mainly by the Americans. It was an attempt to knock out as much of that industry as possible before strategic bombing was halted by the run-up to D-Day and its tactical requirements.

Frankfurt was successfully attacked by over 800 bombers on the night of March 22-23, but a raid on Nürnburg on the last night of the month, although reasonably effective, proved disastrous, 94 aircraft being lost from nearly 800 despatched, the highest loss of any night of the war. The force was a mix of Halifaxes and Lancasters in a proportion of about one to three but the losses of the two types were 17.3 per cent and 11.7 per cent respectively of the total 636 aircraft that attacked the target. No 6 Group, the Canadians, flying both types of bomber, did not find much difference, but No 4 Group, with only 119 Halifaxes had 22 abort and lost another 20. It would appear that the Canadian crews were more highly trained.

This night was a minor victory for the German fighter force which shot down 80 of the bombers, flak claiming the rest. The weather can be blamed for most of the problems, the bombers unusually leaving contrails clearly visible in the moonlight, clouds had dispersed and the wind which had blown them to the target, slowed the homeward journey. The course from the target was marked by wrecked aircraft, a smouldering line across half Germany.

The last raid of the 'Pointblank' offensive was made on heavily defended Munich on April 24-25 to test a new method of low level target marking. 617 Squadron had always done its own pathfinding, and Wing Commander Cheshire, flying a Mosquito VI, was to drop a new pattern flare and, despite heavy flak, flares dropping from above and searchlights, he dived to 700 feet before releasing them successfully. Despite his fuel being short, Cheshire orbited the city at 1,000 feet correcting the bombers' aim, his aircraft suffering much flak damage. For this, and other equally gallant deeds, Wing Commander Cheshire was awarded the VC.

The 'Pointblank' offensive had cost 2,824 aircraft from a total of nearly 75,000 sorties, with more than 20,000 aircrew killed or missing.

Chapter Three

The Lanc as a tactical bomber

When Roy Chadwick designed the Lancaster in 1940, he would have been surprised to know that, by 1944, Barnes Wallis was proposing to modify it for carrying a bomb weighing 22,000 lb or that it would be used for tactical bombing in support of land forces.

In the run up to D-Day, Bomber Command transferred its attention to targets more closely connected with the forthcoming invasion—railways, coastal guns, harbours and airfields, in addition to attacking V-weapon sites. Early in 1944, Harris had been fighting to keep his bombers over industrial targets in Germany but he was over-ruled and, on March 6-7 263 aircraft raided the railway centre at Trappes near Paris putting it out of action for a month. Eight further attacks were made that month on similar targets and the success of the 'Transportation Plan' was assured by the excellent results, and this was approved on April 15.

By the night of June 2-3, when Trappes was again attacked, Bomber Command had dropped over 42,000 tons of bombs in 8,800 sorties with marshalling yards being among 33 railway centres which suffered at their hands. The Région Nord railway network was badly hit and the movement of German troops and material became very difficult, the many detours necessary taking time and, with intruders attacking by day, movements were limited to night hours. Two hundred heavy bombers were lost in these raids but, when June 6 arrived, the railway system could not be used for bringing up reinforcements.

Even Harris had to agree that the Plan had worked, the targets were easily identified using H_2S, pathfinders, operating with a Master Bomber, marked successfully and Lancasters of No 5 Group literally plastered their targets even though the Germans managed to jam their radios and night fighters were active. Ammunition dumps in the invasion area also received attention, five major complexes being destroyed in May, starting with the Toulouse 'Powder Factory' blown up on the first of that month.

Strategic raids on German targets were interspersed depending on the weather, Brunswick, Munich and Schweinfurt receiving attention late in April, the latter again proving to be a 'difficult' target and escaping serious damage.

May 3 saw 362 bombers attacking Mailly le Camp, south of Chalons-sur-Marne, the headquarters of the 21st Panzer Division and a training and repair depot. Forty-two bombers were lost but the target was severely damaged. The force was routed out over Beachy Head at 12,000 feet and descended to a bombing height of 5,000 feet after passing Dieppe and orbited 15 miles from the target whilst the Pathfinders marked the

Roy Chadwick, Sir Stafford and Lady Cripps, with Mr. C.L. Hatton, viewing 'S' for Sugar's nose section at Bracebridge Heath.

The Armstrong-Whitworth-built RE172 demonstrates its camouflage pattern.

barracks. Wing Commander Deane, main force controller, of No 83 Squadron, attempted to call in the 140 Lancasters from No 5 Group but the transmissions were swamped by a powerful but unexpected US broadcast and it was 30 minutes before a clear RT channel could be found and smoke covered the target. The crews at their lower altitude had their Lancasters tossed about by shock waves!

Raids on gun positions split open thick concrete casements, destroyed guns and put equipment out of action so, on D-Day, only one coastal battery was still in action. Signals stations had been destroyed and, once again, Harris's boys had been successful in their task and the enemy's communications in the landing area were 95 per cent wrecked by several small but concentrated Lancaster raids.

The night of June 6 saw a heavy raid on Caen marshalling yards, whilst Pathfinder Lancasters of No 617 Squadron and Stirlings of No 218 Squadron took part in Operation 'Taxable'. During the previous month, the two units had been practising for this

difficult task, that of emulating two large, 7-knot convoys crossing the Channel! Cruising at a steady 200 mph at 3,000 feet, two lines of four aircraft spaced two miles apart, with seven miles between the lines, were to fly on course for 35 seconds, then all turn through 180° and back track for 32 seconds, before repeating the circuit, dropping 'window' at intervals of 12 seconds. On partly jammed enemy radar screens, this gave an accurate simulation of shipping, but the difficulties of accurate flying can be imagined, especially when the first eight aircraft were relieved at 0300 hours! Some 50 hours of practising paid off, German coastal batteries opening up on the ghost fleet using radar prediction!

It was then back to work again, blasting road and rail bridges to stop enemy reinforcements. The 12,000 lb 'Tallboy' penetration bomb was used for the first time on June 9 to block the Saumar railway tunnel and hold up a German Panzer division coming from Bordeaux. The new weapon, developed by Barnes Wallis of Vickers-Armstrong, was 38 inches in diameter and 21 feet 6 inches long with four angled fins to give a slight

Above *A Lancaster of No 467 Squadron with a typical bomb load—4,000 lb 'Cookie', three 1,000-pounders, 12 250-pounders and six incendiary canisters.*
Below *'Ropey', with its shark insignia, at Middleton St George—it was KB772, VR-R, of No 419 Squadron.*

spin, was more of a missile than a bomb. If it could have been dropped from 40,000 feet as designed, it would have hit its target with supersonic speed and penetrated over 100 feet! It fitted snugly into the bomb bay of a Lancaster fitted with specially bulged bomb doors.

The only squadron equipped to carry 'Tallboys' was 617 Squadron then based at Woodhall Spa. Instructions to make the attack were received at 1700 hours, the first of the new weapons having only been delivered two days before! Cheshire, in his Mosquito, dive-bombed from 3,000 feet, landing his red markers in the mouth of the tunnel which took the railway through Saumar Hill and, minutes later, the 12,000 lb bombs were dropping from the Lancasters flying at only 10,000 feet. The crews above were unable to see the results of their attack as the weapons did not explode until they reached nearly 100 feet into the earth, so it was not until a Mosquito reconnaissance aircraft returned with photographs the next morning that their disappointment was turned to awe. One bomb had fallen on the hill and exploded in the tunnel, something like 10,000 tons of earth had been moved and collapsed into the crater, whilst all the other weapons had made craters up to 100 feet across and 70 feet deep! The tunnel had only just been cleared by the time the Allied advance reached the Loire.

Le Havre was raided on June 14 with 617 Squadron flying in at dusk to drop fifteen 'Tallboys' on the E-boat pens. Three of the bombs bored through the concrete roofs and turned the inside into a shambles. Four hundred more Lancasters of Nos 1 and 5 Groups followed up, dropping 1,000 prs and no E-boats escaped. The next night, the dose was repeated at Boulogne, ten 'Tallboys' being dropped and ten being brought home as the crews could not identify the target and had been instructed not to waste the expensive weapon which was also in short supply. 133 small ships, mainly E-boats, were destroyed in the two raids—one cannot say sunk as some were blown right out of the water!

More tactical raids were made at the request of the 21st Army Group, Villers Bocage being attacked on

June 30 by 258 aircraft from Nos 3, 4 and 8 Groups, escorted by nine squadrons of Spitfires. Over 1,000 tons of bombs were dropped with good results, whilst the Caen area was attacked on July 7 and 18, 10,000 tons of bombs being dropped before the army offensives.

Bomber Command again took a hand in the Normandy land battle on July 30, dropping 2,362 tons of bombs in support of the British Second Army south of Caumont, followed by two very heavy raids on the Falaise area, first on August 7-8 and again a fortnight later.

These attacks helped to relieve the pressure on our land forces, Eisenhower describing the spectacle of the mighty air fleets roaring in as having a most heartening effect upon his troops.

The first V-1 flying bombs had been scheduled for launching on December 15 1943 but, due to production and development problems, this date was very much optimistic. The Peenemunde raid in August had not affected V-1 development and it is completely coincidental that intelligence reports had shown the progress with this pilotless reprisal weapon, for, due to its lack of accurate guidance, it could never be more than a nuisance, albeit a deadly one, with its launching sites in northern France. Originally designed for air launching, indeed the first had been tested from a Condor in December 1943, this would not have allowed the weight of attack planned for 5,000 per month (about seven per hour), so a ground launching system had to be developed. This was in the form of a ramp incorporating a steam catapult which boosted the missile to 360 mph to enable the pulse-jet to develop its cruising thrust.

Some 140 of these concrete ramps, each 150 feet long, nicknamed 'ski sites' because of their shape, were detected and all but ten were destroyed in concentrated raids by Bomber Command, the Americans and the Second Tactical Air Force. A simpler, pre-fabricated ramp was quickly developed and first detected by reconnaissance on April 27 and these proved more difficult to trace and destroy. The first bombs were despatched just a week after D-Day and, despite attacks, the launch rate quickly increased to 1,000 per week. Huge concrete roofed underground stores had long been suspected at Watten, Wizernes, Nucourt and Mimoyecques and so 617 Squadron was briefed to attack the first of these, just inland from Calais. Following three days wait due to bad weather, 15 'Tallboy' loaded Lancasters took off from Woodhall Spa on June 19 and climbed to 18,000 feet en route for Watten. Cheshire and Shannon flying at 8,000 feet in their Mosquitos, searched the bomb-scarred area for their target, previous raids having been unsuccessful, whilst 70 guns opened up. Cheshire dived to 2,000 feet to release his smoke markers, these being used by day, but they failed to ignite. Dave Shannon followed and, as he pulled out from his dive, smoke puffs were seen. They had to be near enough as there were no more markers, so Cheshire called in the Lancs. It was the first daylight use of 'Tallboys' and they watched them

spinning in the sunlight, gathering speed and disappearing with a wisp of dust on impact. Barnes Wallis had suggested that the most effective way of using his weapon on this sort of target was to miss by 40 yards!

In the hope that the target had been successfully dealt with, 617 were sent to Wizernes the next day. Here, a huge concrete dome, 20 feet thick was built over a chalk quarry which was later found to be a V-2 rocket store. It was not until June 24 that the second target was attacked, cloud covering the area on the first two sorties. This raid was successful, the face of the quarry disintegrating after five hits! Unfortunately, one Lancaster was lost—the loss rate had fallen sharply after the invasion.

The first V-2 landed on London at 1840 hours on September 8, another fell on Chiswick three minutes later and a third demolished some huts near Epping 16 seconds later. There had been no warning of the attack—the space age had begun! There was no defence, only to attack the suspected launching areas and production lines, especially the fuel source, strikes on liquid oxygen producers being instituted regularly. The rockets were fired from The Hague, from mobile launchers which were difficult to find in the woods and quickly moved! The last rocket aimed at London was fired on March 27 1945, the 1,115th to land on English shores. This was just over 60 per cent of those fired, nearly 8 per cent crashing back on the launching area and the rest malfunctioning during flight.

Meantime, the production line had been located in two parallel tunnels in a former gypsum quarry near Nordhausen in the Harz mountains, a difficult target to attack. 'Tallboys' might have penetrated the mountain, but they were in short supply and reserved for an attack on the *Tirpitz*, whilst 'Grand Slam' had yet to be produced so, other than attacking fuel producers and instrument suppliers, only the firing areas could be dealt with by fighter bombers from the Second Tactical Air Force.

Bomber Command continued its support of the ground forces, dykes were breached in Holland to flood low-lying areas during several raids in October to assist the Canadian Army clear the way to use the port of Antwerp which had fallen on September 4 with its facilities intact, but it was not until the end of November that the estuary had been cleared of mines! Those 'Gardening' sorties were proved to be effective.

Oil and transport targets were the order of the day for the last months of the war, continuing attacks on the Dortmund-Ems Canal keeping this out of commission permanently! As soon as repairs were nearly completed, the Lancs were there again—the German engineers must have been weary with frustration! Pockets of resistance were left to be cleared up, the Germans having fortified French ports which contained 140,000 troops. Eleven thousand were in Le Havre, seven daylight raids were made by Bomber Command from September 5 to 11, a combined force of Halifaxes and Lancasters dropping

9,500 tons of bombs. The port was surrendered to the Canadian First Army on September 12.

Boulogne was next for 'treatment', one raid by Bomber Command on September 17 and continued strikes by medium and fighter-bombers of the Second Tactical Air Force gained its surrender on the 26th. Calais was raided on September 20, 25 and 27, surrendering early in October. In some 6,000 sorties a total of 14 aircraft was lost.

The Germans had started the war with two battleships (*Bismarck* and *Tirpitz*), two battle cruisers (*Scharnhorst* and *Gneisenau*) and three so-called pocket battleships (*Admiral von Scheer, Graf Spee* and *Deutschland—* later *Lützow*). They had been a thorn in our side until their destruction as it was never known when they might break out into the Atlantic to raid convoys in support of the U-boat campaign. Churchill, and their Lordships at the Admiralty, insisted on maximum effort to neutralise this menace, and Bomber Command took a large share of this. The *Graf Spee* and *Deutschland* had slipped into the Atlantic, undetected, a few days before war was declared, the former to be scuttled in the Battle of the River Plate, whilst the latter returned safely to Wilhelmshaven in November in foggy weather. *Scheer* received the first attack of the war on September 4 when Blenheims of 139 Squadron found her in Schillig Roads.

Bismarck, escorted by cruiser *Prinz Eugen*, passed through the Kattegat on May 20 1941 and was found off Bergen by a PRU Spitfire. Leaving the Norwegian fjords, they were next detected between Iceland and Greenland by radar from a surface vessel. The two ships were shadowed from the air and intercepted by *HMS Hood* and *HMS Prince of Wales*. The former was sunk but hits had been made on the *Bismarck* reducing her speed, and a Swordfish from *Ark Royal* crippled her steering to enable surface forces to deliver the coup-de-grâce. The combined efforts of air and sea forces had been successful but *Prinz Eugen* escaped to Brest.

The *Lützow* was torpedoed off Norway on June 13 1941 by Beauforts of No 42 Squadron. Brest received frequent attacks as the two battle cruisers, with *Prinz Eugen*, were holed up, receiving regular repairs to keep them seaworthy after the various raids. The entrance to the port was mined, such raids becoming a nightly routine from December 11 with 101 bombers being involved on the 17th and a raid by 41 Manchesters, Halifaxes and Stirlings, with fighter escort followed the next day, six bombers being lost, but *Gneisenau* was damaged and *Scharnhorst* was trapped for a month by wrecked lock gates. Despite constant attention, all three units left Brest on the evening of February 11 1942, a fact not detected by the RAF for over 12 hours, and successfully escaped through the Channel and arrived at Wilhelmshaven, only *Scharnhorst* receiving any real damage after hitting mines.

Bomber Command had failed to find the ships, but *Gneisenau* suffered two direct hits during a raid on Kiel at the end of February, and *Prinz Eugen* had been damaged by a torpedo at Trondheim a few days earlier after joining up with the *Tirpitz* and *Scheer*. Here the three ships were in a position to attack north Russian convoys and tied up several capital ships, carriers and scores of aircraft. The *Tirpitz* was attacked off Norway and the uncompleted aircraft carrier, *Graf Zeppelin*, received attention where it was being fitted out at Gdynia, from where it never moved.

Trondheimfjord eventually became the home for the remaining German capital ships, *Hipper, Scheer* and *Tirpitz*. Here they were to pose a threat to the Russian convoys, especially the ill-fated PQ 17 which, though not attacked by the German ships, their threat caused the withdrawal of heavy escort vessels and hence the nigh-destruction of the defenceless merchantmen.

The first series of raids on the heavily camouflaged *Tirpitz*, moored under the sloping side of the mountain at the head of the fjord, was made at the end of March and in April 1942, by Yorkshire-based Halifaxes. On the night of April 27-28, Nos 10 and 76 Squadrons were to bomb with 4,000 lb bombs from 4,000 feet, these to be followed by No 35 Squadron whose Halifaxes were each to drop four modified sea mines from masthead height. It was hoped that these could be dropped down the cliff face within the protecting anti-torpedo nets.

10 Squadron's commanding officer, Wing Commander D.C.T. Bennett, was shot down but, luckily, he escaped through Sweden and was home inside five weeks, to battle for the Pathfinder Force which he eventually formed. The only extant Halifax, W1048, TL-S, of 35 Squadron, on its first raid, was hit in its starboard wing and crash-landed on the ice of nearby Lake Hoklingen, eventually to sink through into 90 feet of water and be salvaged for the Royal Air Force Museum in 1973.

Tirpitz was seriously damaged in an attack by miniature submarines in Kaalfjord on September 22 1943 and it was not until April 3 1944 that it was thought necessary to make a further attack. The Fleet Air Arm mounted an attack from six carriers, the repaired *Tirpitz* being ready for steaming trials in Altenfjord. 42 Barracuda dive-bombers, in two groups, escorted by 80 fighters, Corsairs, Hellcats, Seafires and Wildcats, made a surprise attack. Fifteen direct hits by 500 and 1,000 lb bombs, all dropped in two minutes, and additional damage from near misses, postponed the running trials for some time! A further raid was made by 45 Barracudas, escorted by 50 Corsairs, flying from three carriers, *Formidable, Indefatigable* and *Furious*, but this time the Germans were ready. Following the earlier raid, hilltop lookouts had been organised and a radar station erected, so the Barracudas found the fjord filled with artificial smoke, and could not pinpoint their target.

Further attacks were made by carrier aircraft on August 22 and the following three days, it being hoped that the smoke-screen could not be kept up for a period. Results were again disappointing, the only direct hit failing to explode. At this point it was decided that Bomber Command should have another try and so 617

Squadron was ordered to make an attack with their 'Tallboys' which were now available in sufficient quantities to warrant their use. However, the range was prohibitive, 3,000 miles total! The decision to fly from Russia was made, the trip was 1,750 miles with 2,000 gallons of petrol and the 12,000 lb bombs, but the final raid would only be 600 miles each way. Hence, on September 10, with No 9 Squadron, 617 set off on this longest flight with a bomb load, some 11 to 12 hours in the air. To make matters worse, weather conditions deteriorated on the way, the Yagodnik radio beacon proved to be the wrong kind, and many Lancasters were lost although the two Liberators with ground crews and spares arrived safely. Most of the missing machines had landed elsewhere and the Russians quickly rounded them up, only six which landed in the marshes being lost.

The weather stayed bad and it was not until September 15 that a Mosquito weather aircraft reported Altenfjord was clear. 28 Lancasters were quickly in the air and heading west, flying low over the White Sea to avoid detection. Climbing to 11,000 feet, Tait was the first to bomb but the smoke screen was spreading and Daniels, in the nose of his aircraft, resorted to guesswork, others aimed at the flashes from the many AA guns, and some landed back at Yagodnik with their 'Tallboys' still in place. Everyone was disappointed and it was not until later that a Norwegian reported a great hole in the forward deck. *Tirpitz* had disappeared from her fjord and it was some time before she was found at Tromsö for repairs—Tait's bomb-aimer had scored a lucky hit! Even more important, she was 200 miles nearer to Scottish bases, so there was a chance of another raid if 300 gallons more fuel could be carried!

During this period, another dam had come up, the American armies being held on the Rhine at the Belfort Gap near the Swiss border near the Kembs Dam. Here the flood gates could be blown up to release an enormous amount of water that would sweep away any American assault forces—unless this could be released earlier! A job for the Dam Busters, but their Lancasters had been modified back to standard and it would take weeks to carry out the earlier Type 464 provisioning. Bombing from altitude could not be accurate enough so could a 'Tallboy' be dropped from low level to slide into the water until it hit the gate, sticking in the concrete before exploding by a delayed fuse? There was no time for a trial, so 617 got the job to try it for real!

By splitting the squadron, a formation would bomb from 8,000 feet, it was hoped keeping the flak-gunners occupied, whilst six Lancasters would sneak in at low level and a squadron of Mustangs would strafe the area. Timing was of the utmost importance and a week was given over to practising. October 7 was fixed for the raid, a bright sunny day with low, broken cloud. One Lancaster flew too near Switzerland and was hit in its starboard engine by neutral AA fire. Timing was perfect, ground fire being concentrated on the Lancasters bombing from above whilst the Mustangs

dived out of the sun and Tait skimmed down the Rhine and dropped his bomb which headed for the right hand sluice-gate. Two other Lancasters were shot out of the sky on their run-in and this was the only hit. The delay was set for 30 minutes and a Mosquito watched as the sluice-gate burst and a huge torrent of water poured forth, barges even in Switzerland grounding as the pent-up waters of the Rhine dispersed.

With this essential tactical interruption, it was back to the *Tirpitz*. To carry the extra fuel, long cylindrical tanks as used for fitting in the bomb bays of Wellingtons were sought and collected from all over the country. These could be threaded into the Lancaster's fuselage and, with Mosquito long-range tanks, increased the fuel load by the amount required. This introduced another problem—taking off at nearly 2 tons overweight! It was agreed that, providing the more powerful Merlin 24 could be fitted to 617's Lancasters, this was an acceptable risk. The records of 5 Group were studied and with sufficient of the 1,610 HP Merlins (220 hp more than usual) located, the immense task of exchanging engines within three days was put in hand. The same modifications were made to 9 Squadron's aircraft by ground crews working night and day in continuous dense fog.

The weather was critical as the long winter nights started at Tromsö before the end of November, giving a dead-line to be met, and the prevailing westerly wind kept blowing cloud over the target. A Mosquito signalled the wind veering to the east on October 28, so the waiting Lancasters took off from their Lincolnshire bases for Lossiemouth. The bombers took off at 0100 hours, their Merlins straining at full emergency power, keeping low over the sea, then climbing over Norway towards Sweden for an attack from the east with mountains shielding the Lancasters from Tromsö radar.

At the last moment, the wind changed and cloud blew over Altenfjord, so the 'Tallboys' were again dropped blindly, and no hits were recorded although there were some near misses. A disappointing raid, but all Lancasters save one, which crash landed in a Swedish bog with two engines out, returned to their home bases.

Another wait for favourable weather was enforced and on November 4 the force flew north to Lossiemouth only to return to Woodhall the next morning when a gale blew up. It was learned that a squadron of German fighters had been moved to Bardufoss, only 50 kilometres from Tromsö—the reason was obvious! A week passed before the weather forecasters saw a change, so off to Lossiemouth again—it was getting monotonous. However, at 0300 hours on November 12, the two squadrons were airborne again, their 32-ton aircraft struggling to leave the ground.

Dawn was breaking when the Lancasters, flying at 14,000 feet, approached from the south-east—and saw the ship clearly nestling in her torpedo nets. No fighters appeared and 617 bombed first, followed by 9 Squadron still using their Mk XIV bomb-sights. Flak opened up but the bombs were already on their half minute drop,

A Lancaster B1 modified to carry a 'Grand Slam'—Note its neat fitting (Roy Cross).

and they hit, first the battleship's foredeck, then her starboard side near the bridge and then abaft her funnel. The fighters were too late, *Tirpitz* turned over, the end of the story.

Ironically, the last two attacks were unnecessary, the single hit on September 15 having damaged the ship beyond repair and she had been towed to Tromsö not for repair but to be used as an unsinkable fortress. Unfortunately, the water was not shallow enough and, although the sea bed was being filled underneath the battleship, this was too late.

A permanent memorial to the efforts of the two successful Lancaster squadrons still remains at Kaafjord, two enormous craters made by 'Tallboy' bombs, one of them straight in the middle of the narrow spit of land to

which the *Tirpitz* was moored. The Kaafjord is surrounded by mountains and, among these, on the east side, is another crater, 30 feet deep in solid rock, surely a fitting tribute to the work of Barnes Wallis.

By the beginning of 1945, German fighter resistance was crumbling and the Lancaster was used more and more by day, even 617 Squadron, with its reduced armament, was wrecking U-boat pens from Bergen to Ijmuiden, suitable targets for their 'Tallboys' being difficult to find. With the Dortmund-Ems Canal permanently drained, Eisenhower requested an all-out assault on the German railway system so that areas thus isolated could be dealt with one by one. The Bielefeld Viaduct, near Bremen, was the main link between the Ruhr and north-west Germany, so had been the subject

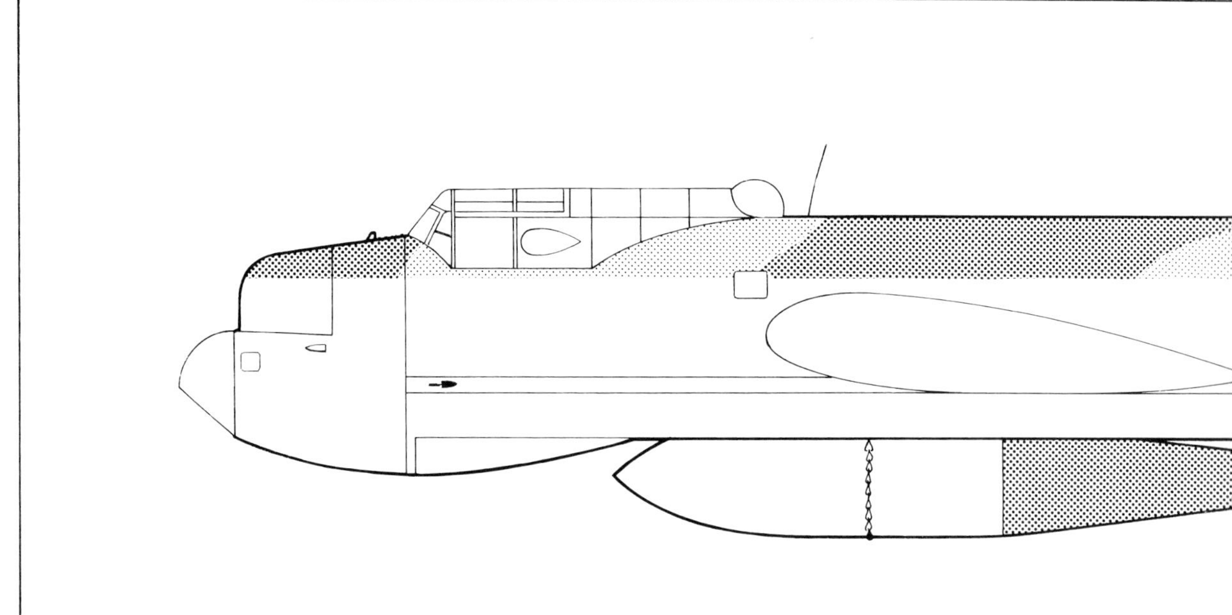

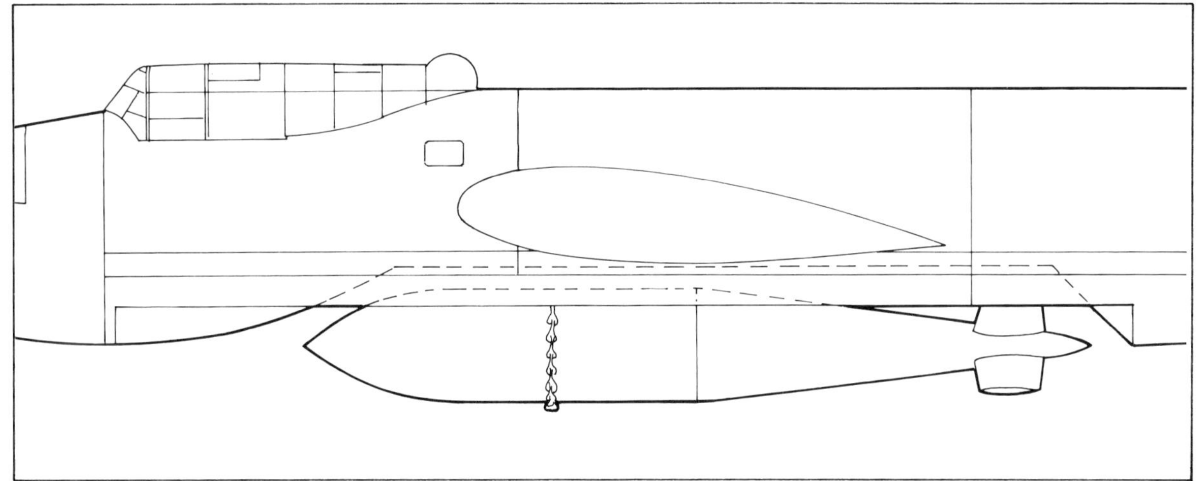

The 22,000 lb 'Grand Slam'.

of many raids, but 3,000 tons of bombs had done no more than crater the surrounding marshes. 617 was called in to give specialist treatment and, on the third attempt, dropped 'Tallboys' from 18,000 feet—without noticeable effect!

'Grand Slam' had been in production for some months, despite difficulties in finding suitable steel for casting the huge casing which weighed ten tons before machining. The first two were delivered to Woodhall Spa on March 13 1945 and loaded on two specially modified Lancasters the next morning. Fitted with the most powerful Merlins and with fuselages, undercarriages and bomb beams strengthened, bomb-doors removed and fairings fitted in the front and rear

of the bomb bay, these Lancasters were to carry the new weapon, the 'earthquake' bomb, first envisaged by Barnes Wallis in 1939! Only one of the two Lancasters was serviceable, so this staggered off the ground with the rest of the squadron equipped with 'Tallboys'.

Thirty-five seconds after being released, the new bomb hit the ground only 30 yards from the Bielefeld Viaduct, exploding at a depth of about 100 feet some ten seconds later. The marsh erupted, throwing debris 500 feet into the air, and a hundred yards of the viaduct just disappeared into the crater! Several more of the 22,000 lb bombs were delivered that month. Five destroyed the Arnsberg Viaduct on March 19, the Arbergen and Nienburg Bridges receiving similar treatment on March

The Lancaster B1 Special fitted with 'Grand Slam'.

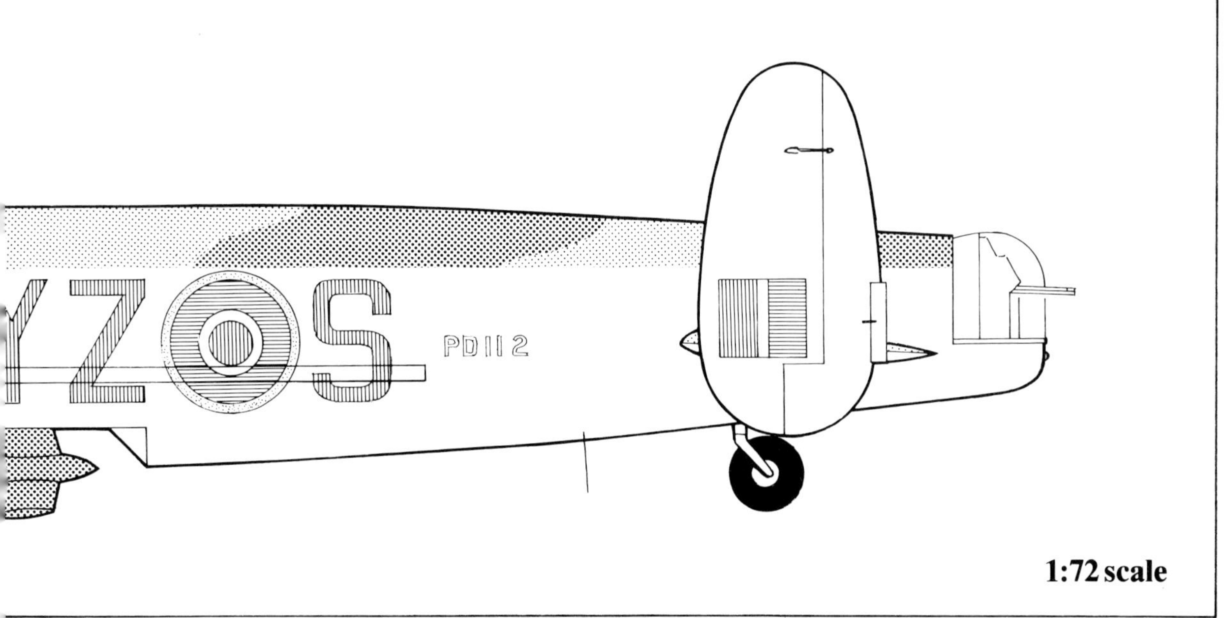

21 and 22 respectively. The last railway bridge still serving the Ruhr was hit by two 'Grand Slams' and two 'Tallboys' the next day and that was the end of this type of target!

One pocket battleship, the *Lützow*, remained and this was sheltering at Swinemünde in the Baltic, so 617 Squadron set out on April 13 to attend to it, but the area was covered with cloud as it was again two days later. The following day, this time with an escort of long-range fighters, 617 found the area clear and heavy flak awaiting them. All but two of the 18 Lancasters were hit, one spun down over the target, but at least three hits were seen before smoke covered the ship. When reconnaissance photos arrived, *Lützow* looked intact and it was not until two days later that 617 found out she had sunk at her moorings, a near miss having torn out her bottom at the bows and she was resting in shallow mud.

Heligoland was next for treatment, half at a time, ending the blockade of the approaches to the north-west ports. 617's last operation, on April 25, was to the Eagle's Nest at Berchtesgaden, but deep snow covered the area hiding the target, so four 'Tallboys' and a selection of 1,000-pounders flattened the nearby SS barracks, a more worthwhile target.

Bomber Command, during the early months of 1945, concentrated on oil plants both by night and day and, by April, fuel production was negligible although most of the damage had been wrought 12 months earlier. Dresden was raided twice in one night in the middle of February by a total of 773 Lancasters in support of the Russian advance, as it was thought to be a centre of communications. The lovely old town was completely destroyed and it will never be known how many casualties were caused as it was full of refugees.

Lancasters were out every night when the weather was suitable, attacking oil refineries, marshalling yards and shipyards, the Blohm and Voss U-boat yards in Hamburg receiving special attention, until the night of May 2-3, the last night attack of the war, when Kiel was the target.

During the last four years of World War 2, Lancasters had taken off on over 156,000 sorties, 100,000 had attacked by night, 35,000 by day, over 600,000 tons of bombs had been dropped from a total of 955,000 tons by all types, 3,349 had failed to return from operations and 487 were damaged.

Above *A No 617 Squadron Lancaster, YZ-J, being loaded with a 'Grand Slam' at Woodhall Spa.*

Below *H_2S equipped PD235, OL-N^2 of No 83 Squadron, looks 'new'.*

Chapter Four

Development

As already recorded, the prototype Lancaster was a modified Manchester, the basic fuselage of all production aircraft being changed only in detail. Internally, more alterations would be found and it is perhaps true to say that the Lancaster and radar were developed concurrently and this was the only factor to alter greatly the basic silhouette when the H_2S ventral radome was added.

One notable addition in the cockpit area was the incorporation of a Flight Engineer into the crew. He sat just aft of where the Second Pilot would have sat had one been carried (a small number of Lancs had dual control for conversion training), facing his panel which was mounted on the starboard fuselage wall. Engine instruments were duplicated but, in addition, fuel gauges and tank selection were the Flight Engineer's responsibility. His close proximity to the navigator was a big help when operating at the longer ranges!

Like the Manchester, a row of shallow windows, fitted with curtains, was a noticeable feature of early Lancasters but these were later deleted. The dorsal twin .303 in Browning FN 50 turret was originally unfaired but this was later modified to have a prominent fairing incorporating a cam ring to guard the Lanc's structure from being shot away in the heat of combat!

The 33-foot long, full width bomb-bay was to lend itself to much adaption for fitting bigger and more beautiful bombs. Initially this was done by bulging the double bomb doors, but these were deleted completely when the 22,000 lb 'Grand Slam' was carried, although one Lancaster (PP741) had special doors fitted experimentally. Like the cylindrical mine, Dambusting Lancs, fairings were fitted in the bomb-bay to keep drag to a minimum. At the beginning of hostilities, the largest bombs available were 1,000-pounders, but these were stepped up to 2,000 lb, armour piercing, general purpose or high capacity, 4,000 and 8,000 lb block-busters, the latter being built up from two 4,000-pounders. The 12,000 lb streamlined 'Tallboy' was completely enclosed in use, and six 1,500 lb sea mines were an alternative load.

Armament varied only slightly, the FN 5 nose turret was a common fitment, unless it was deleted and faired over to save weight as in the B 1 (Special). Several different types of tail turrets were fitted, early ones with four .303 in Browning—the Manchester had a Nash and Thomson Type 'X' which was replaced in early Lancasters with the FN 20 with reflector gun sight. This

can be identified by the complete structure to support the guns as this passes up and over the gunner. During 1943, the FN 120 was introduced, this having improved vision, the gun support framework being much reduced, with windows down the front of the cupola and sliding side windows. A series 2 FN 120 was introduced with modification to take AGL (T) (Village Inn radar sighting) but this was not fitted, a Mk II gyro gun sight being used. The FN 121 did, however, have AGL (T), a Mk IIc gyro gun sight and electric servo feed.

Twin .5 in Colt-Brownings were used in later aircraft, first fitted in the Rose type 'R' No 2 Mk I turret. Developed by Rose Bros in Gainsborough, this turret

Above *The morning after—Canadian crew members view damage to BII DS686, OW-F of No 426 Squadron.*

Below *The Flight Engineer's panel on the starboard cockpit wall (A.V. Roe Ltd).*

The production line of Victory Aircraft, Malton, January 28 1944.

was much more roomy than the FN 20 which it was designed to replace in just $3\frac{1}{2}$ hours without modification to the mounting. Tank fed, each gun had 335 rounds, it could rotate through 188°, with 49° elevation and 59° depression but, more important, the gunner could bale out quickly and easily between the widely spaced guns. The hitting power of the bigger guns gave better results, a range of 600 yards being common and the effectiveness of a short burst (as low as 17 rounds recorded in one 'kill') was surprising. Very few squadrons had this turret fitted, most being close to the maker's works as they were developed during their service trials!

The Mk VII Lancaster was designed for twin .5 in guns in the tail, these being fitted in the newly developed FN 82 turret, with provision for AGL (T), also used in the later Lincoln, originally designated Lancaster IV.

It was planned to fit later Lancasters with a Martin mid-upper turret, also having .5 in guns, further forward than was standard and placed over the bomb bay. 50 Mk 1s were built by Austin Motors with the normal Frazer Nash turret in the forward position but its bulk blocked the walk-way making these Lancasters unpopular in service! Another Lancaster, JB456, was experimentally fitted with the Bristol B17 turret having two 20 mm cannon and this was later adopted for the Lincoln.

The fitting of the ventral turret, the twin .303 in periscope sighted FN 64, sometimes faired into the back of the bulged bomb doors, was the subject of much discussion. First used in the Manchester, many crews thought that it was unnecessary and had it removed,

'Titus' a B II, DS845, of No 408 (Goose) Squadron, at Linton-on-Ouse in 1943.

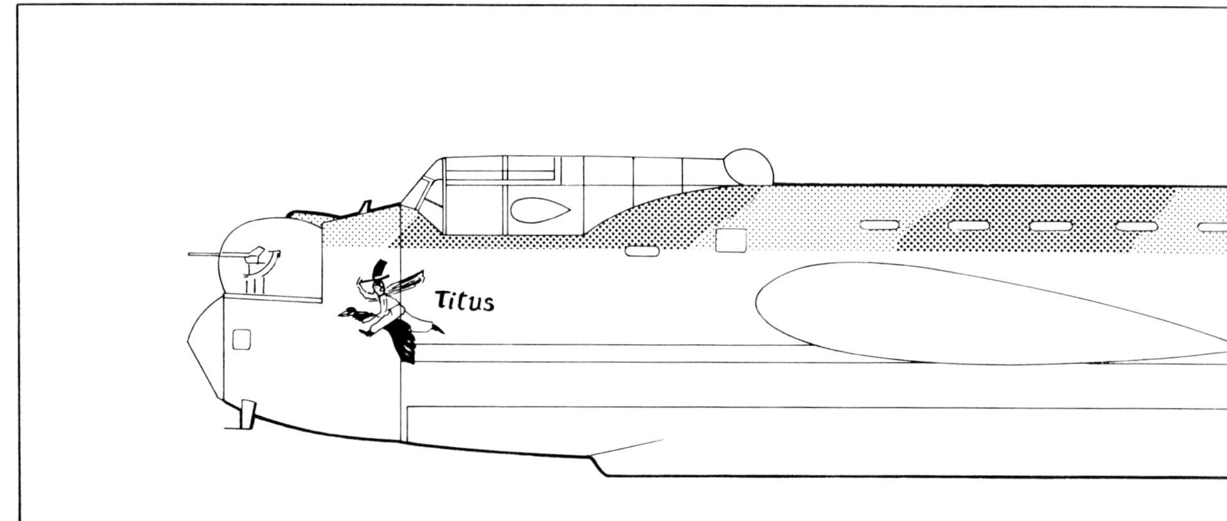

A line up of repaired noses.

others made their own experiments with cannon, .5 in or .303 in machine guns. Certainly a defence against the night fighters equipped with 'Schrage Musik' upward firing cannon was required but, usually, after a careful stalking, their targets were shot out of the sky without sufficient warning to retaliate.

Another trial, with two Lancasters, was the fitting of 20 mm cannon in remotely controlled dorsal and ventral barbettes. These were sighted from a rear aiming position.

Many Lancasters, including the Dam Busters and 'Grand Slam' aircraft, had their mid-upper turrets removed and blanked over to save weight, this modification being incorporated in most post-war maritime reconnaissance aircraft even though weight was no longer a problem.

When H_2S plan-position radar was fitted, the moulded perspex scanner blister was installed just behind the bomb-bay and the ventral turret mount was deleted. The streamline perspex dome was sprayed over with matt black paint, a portion at the rear being left clear as it covered the downward identification lights, three of which were mounted in the rear fuselage.

One of the external features which distinguishes the Mk III Lancaster is the enlarged nose dome fitted to allow the use of the SABS bomb sight. It is $7\frac{1}{2}$ inches deeper than the earlier nose window, but both have the $20\frac{13}{16}$ inches diameter optical flat panel for the air bomber and is $\frac{5}{16}$ inch nominal thickness instead of $\frac{3}{16}$ inch.

Unfortunately, this is not the main reason for the designation change and, as Mk 1 and Mk III Lancasters were built more or less side-by-side until the end of the war, and could also have their type changed on the squadron simply by an engine swap, it leads to much confusion. All Mk III Lancasters were to have been fitted with Packard built Merlin 28 or 38 engines of 1,390 hp as opposed to the XX or 22 of similar power

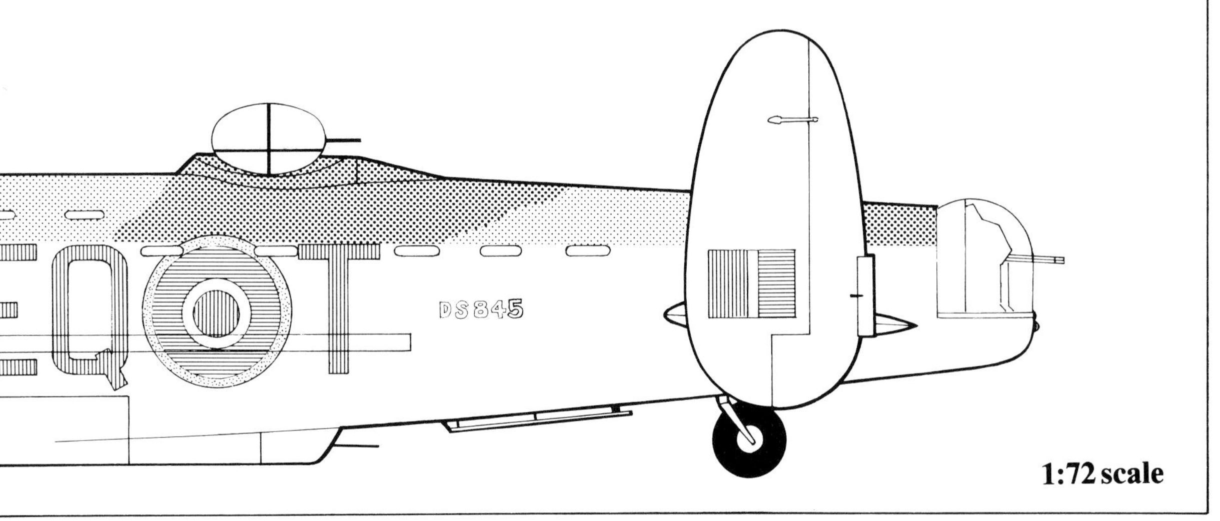

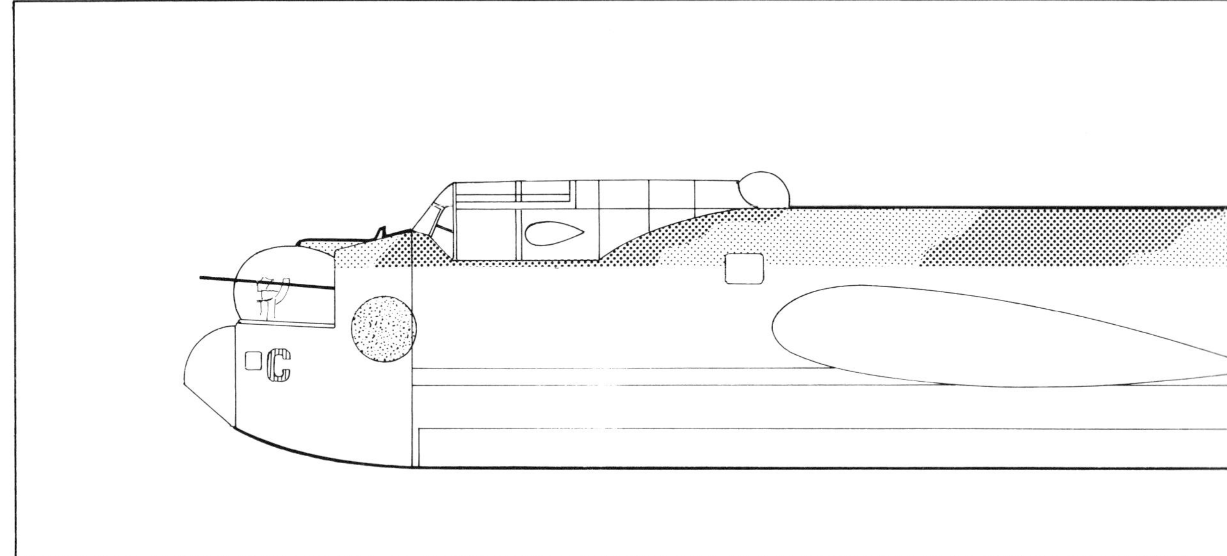

No 170 Squadron's TC-C, LM732, with Rose tail turret.

Below *B III air bomber's position—retrofitted on some B1s!*

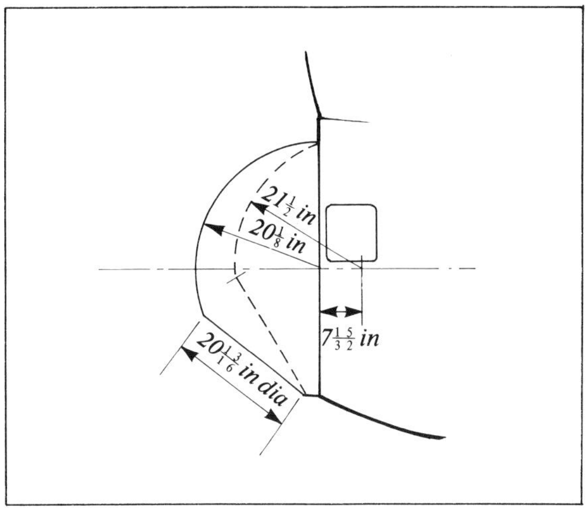

fitted to the Mk 1. Both types could have Merlin 24 or Packard Merlin 224 engines of 1,610 hp fitted, these being the types fitted to the B1 (Special). Major difference between the Merlin XX and the 22 is the use of a two-piece cylinder block, the head being made and bolted on separately to facilitate production. All the Merlins fitted had a bore and stroke of 5.4 inches and 6 inches respectively, giving a capacity of 27 litres (1,647 cubic inches—hence the American designation V-1650, the V indicating the cylinder layout, two banks of six cylinders arranged in a Vee). Dry weight was 1,450-1,460 lb and two-speed superchargers were fitted maintaining power up to 10-11,000 feet.

With the fear that Merlins might become in short supply due to enemy action, (Rolls-Royce's Derby factory, surprisingly, only suffered one air attack on July 27 1942!), Avro's investigated the fitting of Bristol Hercules VI or XVI engines as used in the Short Stirling and later marks of Halifax. Fitted with Mk VI engines of 1,650 hp (again Beaufighter engines had to be utilised!), DT810 was quickly converted at Chadderton and first flew on November 26 1941, being tested at Boscombe Down early the next year. The interchangeable Hercules 'Power Egg' had been fully tested and no problems were encountered, so a production contract for 300 Lancaster B Mk IIs was placed with Armstrong Whitworth Aircraft at Baginton. They had continued the building of Whitleys following cancellation of the Manchester contract for which they had tooled up, so were able to complete the first two aircraft, DS601/2, in September 1942 and these were allotted to Boscombe Down for trials along with DS606 later.

With extra power, nearly 1,000 hp from all four engines, performance was expected to be improved, but the 52 inch diameter, 18-cylinder, two row, sleeve valve, aircooled radial engine, with bore and stroke of $5\frac{3}{4}$ inches and $6\frac{1}{2}$ inches and capacity of 38.7 litres (2,360 cubic in) was much heavier at around 1,900 lb and very much thirstier! These factors, along with increased drag, lowered the operational ceiling of the Lancaster B Mk II and cut its bomb load.

The first production aircraft were issued to No 61 Squadron at Syerston, Nottinghamshire, for service trials and comparison with the Merlin engined Lancasters already used by this unit. From mid-October 1942, for four months, the Hercules was on trial and it failed miserably, very few of the tasks set being accomplished. The standard Lancaster usually attained 22,000 feet over the target, whereas the B Mk IIs very rarely achieved 5,000 feet below this! Despite all the problems encountered, all nine Lancasters survived and were handed over to No 115 Squadron at East Wretham in Norfolk, the first unit to have them allocated—No 5 Group was pleased to be rid of them!

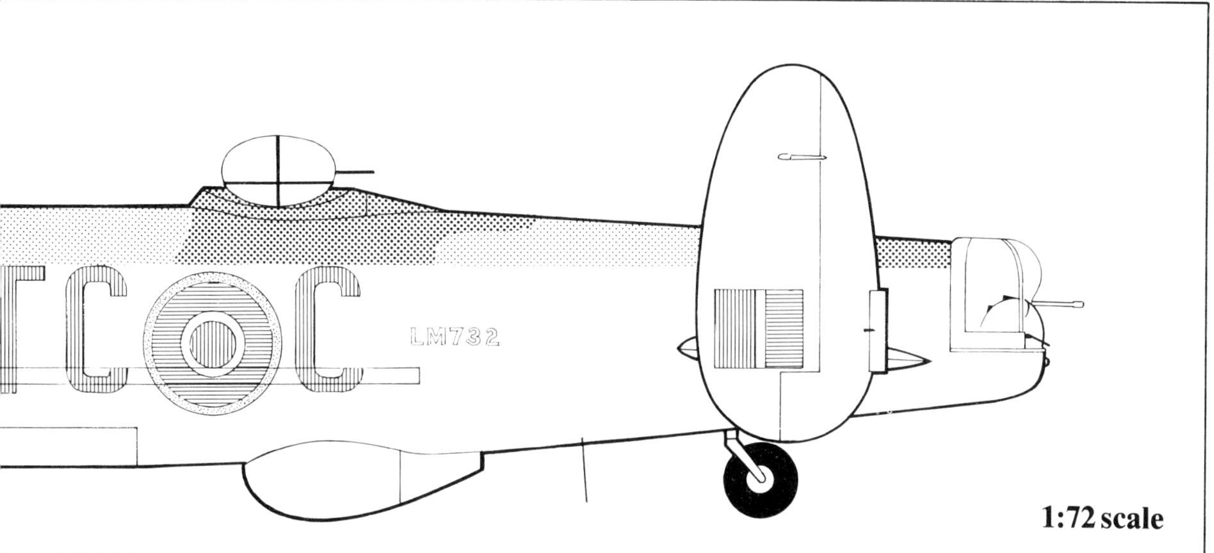

1:72 scale

The Lancaster Group was responsible for all production, and comprised the A.V. Roe factories at Manchester and Yeadon, Metropolitan-Vickers also at Manchester, Vickers Armstrong at Chester and Castle Bromwich, Austin Motors at Longbridge, Victory Aircraft at Malton in Canada and Armstrong Whitworth Aircraft at Baginton, Bitteswell and Sywell. Dispersal of production was carried to the limit and it is interesting to note the types of factories which became involved.

Components for Armstrong Whitworth's 300 Mk IIs were manufactured in various places, the fuselage, centre section and nose sections were first assembled in the Corporation Tram Sheds in Northampton, whilst Pearce's Shoe Factory built tail sections! The wings were made at Baginton by Armstrong Whitworth themselves and some 100 aircraft were assembled at Sywell, their components having been brought in by road. The first was test-flown there by Wing Commander Charles Turner-Hughes ('Toc H' of pre-war aerobatic fame) on July 31 1942, and the last on November 25 1943.

Three RCAF squadrons in No 6 Group, waiting their Canadian built Mk Xs were equipped with the B Mk II. They were No 408 (Goose) and No 426 (Thunderbird) at Linton-on-Ouse, and No 432 (Leaside) at East Moor, all in No 6 Group in Yorkshire. The only other squadron to use the Hercules Lancaster was No 514 at Foulsham, Norfolk and Waterbeach, Cambridgeshire, in 3 Group like No 115 Squadron.

The majority of Lancaster B Mk IIs were fitted with the FN 64 ventral turret and bulged bomb doors of two distinct types, capable of enclosing an 8,000 lb block-buster bomb among its 14,000 bomb load, a reduction of 4,000 lb from the standard Merlin aircraft having been found essential. H_2S was not fitted on the Hercules Lancaster.

Early Lancaster B Mk IIs had Stirling-type air intakes, later replaced by the short type as used on the Beaufighter. Propeller blade line was only $\frac{5}{8}$ inch behind that of the Merlin, but the centre line was 14 inches lower (Vulture and Merlin had the same centre line, $8\frac{1}{8}$ inches above datum line-top of flight deck floor).

The only other major engine to be used was in the Lancaster VI which had Merlin 68/85 Universal power plants with circular cowlings as later used on the Lincoln. These engines developed 1,635 hp but perhaps more important, they maintained power 5,000 feet higher than earlier versions, although they were 200 lb heavier. Only one squadron, No 635 at Wyton, was to use this Lancaster mark, having seven of the eight aircraft converted in 1944 by Rolls-Royce at Hucknall (see Chapter 5).

By 1944, the operational Lancaster was loaded with both offensive and defensive radar/radio, now collectively known as electronics. Besides Gee, G-H, IFF, H_2S, Village Inn, Monica and Mandril, one

Below *A Merlin 22 engine* (Rolls-Royce Ltd).

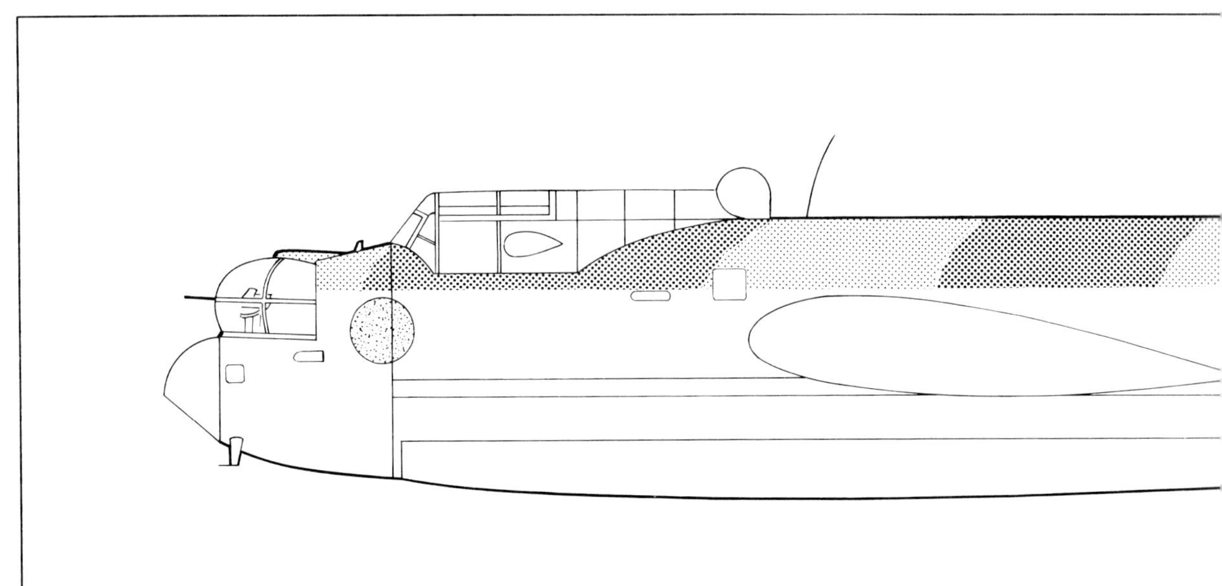

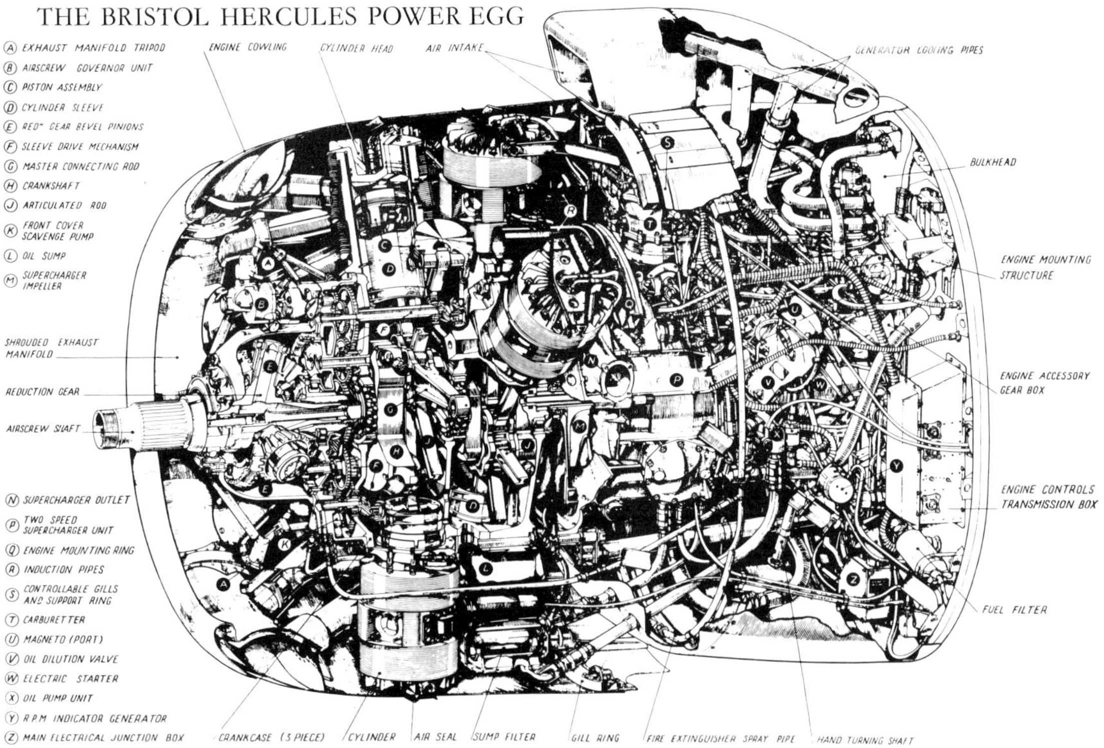

THE BRISTOL HERCULES POWER EGG

(A) EXHAUST MANIFOLD TRIPOD
(B) AIRSCREW GOVERNOR UNIT
(C) PISTON ASSEMBLY
(D) CYLINDER SLEEVE
(E) REDⁿ GEAR BEVEL PINIONS
(F) SLEEVE DRIVE MECHANISM
(G) MASTER CONNECTING ROD
(H) CRANKSHAFT
(J) ARTICULATED ROD
(K) FRONT COVER SCAVENGE PUMP
(L) OIL SUMP
(M) SUPERCHARGER IMPELLER

SHROUDED EXHAUST MANIFOLD
REDUCTION GEAR
AIRSCREW SHAFT

(N) SUPERCHARGER OUTLET
(P) TWO SPEED SUPERCHARGER UNIT
(Q) ENGINE MOUNTING RING
(R) INDUCTION PIPES
(S) CONTROLLABLE GILLS AND SUPPORT RING
(T) CARBURETTER
(U) MAGNETO (PORT)
(V) OIL DILUTION VALVE
(W) ELECTRIC STARTER
(X) OIL PUMP UNIT
(Y) R.P.M INDICATOR GENERATOR
(Z) MAIN ELECTRICAL JUNCTION BOX

ENGINE COWLING — CYLINDER HEAD — AIR INTAKE — GENERATOR COOLING PIPES — BULKHEAD — ENGINE MOUNTING STRUCTURE — ENGINE ACCESSORY GEAR BOX — ENGINE CONTROLS TRANSMISSION BOX — FUEL FILTER

CRANKCASE (3 PIECE) — CYLINDER — AIR SEAL — SUMP FILTER — GILL RING — FIRE EXTINGUISHER SPRAY PIPE — HAND TURNING SHAFT

HERCULEAN. A detailed sectional drawing by the Bristol Aeroplane Co. Ltd. showing the complete "power egg" and the accessories included with the engine itself as a single unit.

Left *A Hercules VI-powered Lancaster II.*

Above *A Bristol Hercules Power Egg.*

Below *PA220, a B III of No 300 Squadron, with H$_2$S, 4,000 lb bomb doors and white codes.*

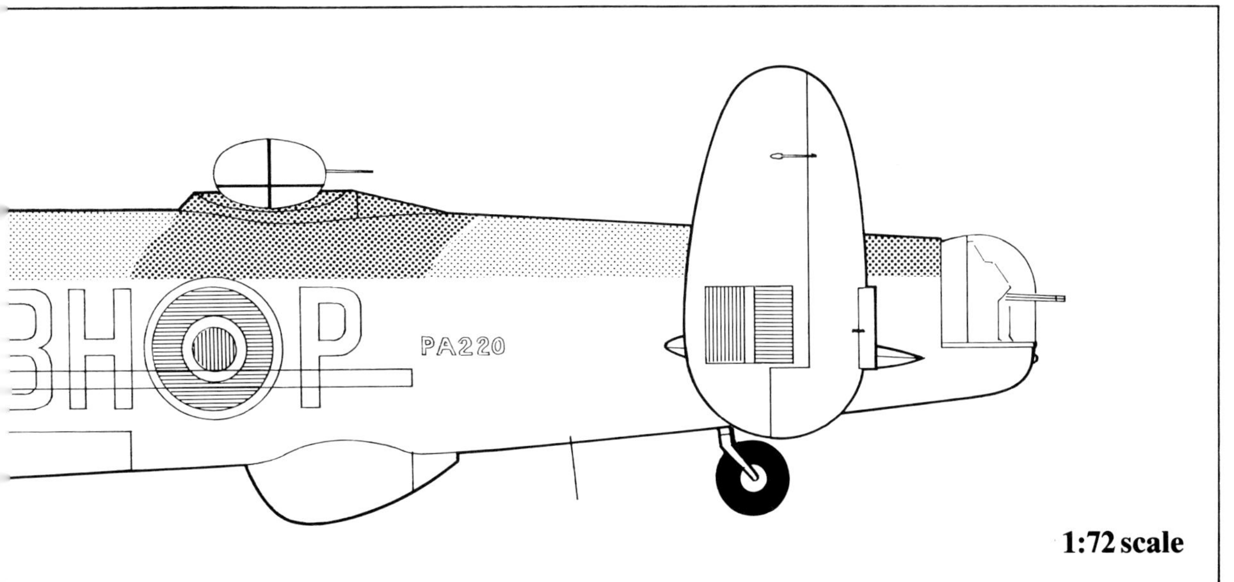

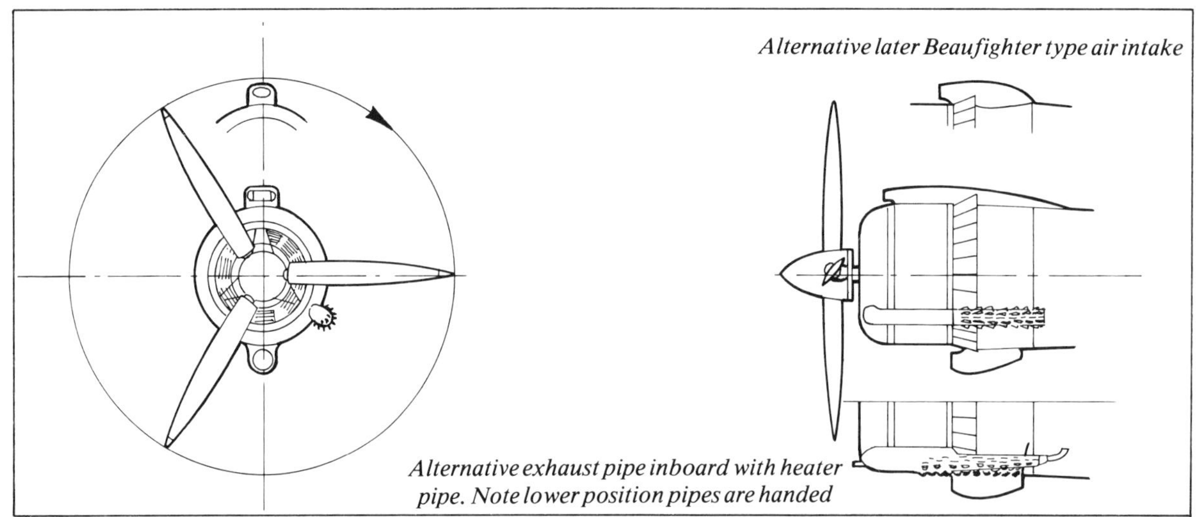

Above *Port Hercules Power Egg.*

Below *Lancaster noses on the production line—tails can be seen behind* (Hawker Siddeley Ltd).

Bottom *Wing tips being repaired by Brush Coachworks at their Loughborough works.*

Above *A snug-fitting airborne lifeboat at St Eval in 1952.*

Below *The Mk II airborne lifeboat.*

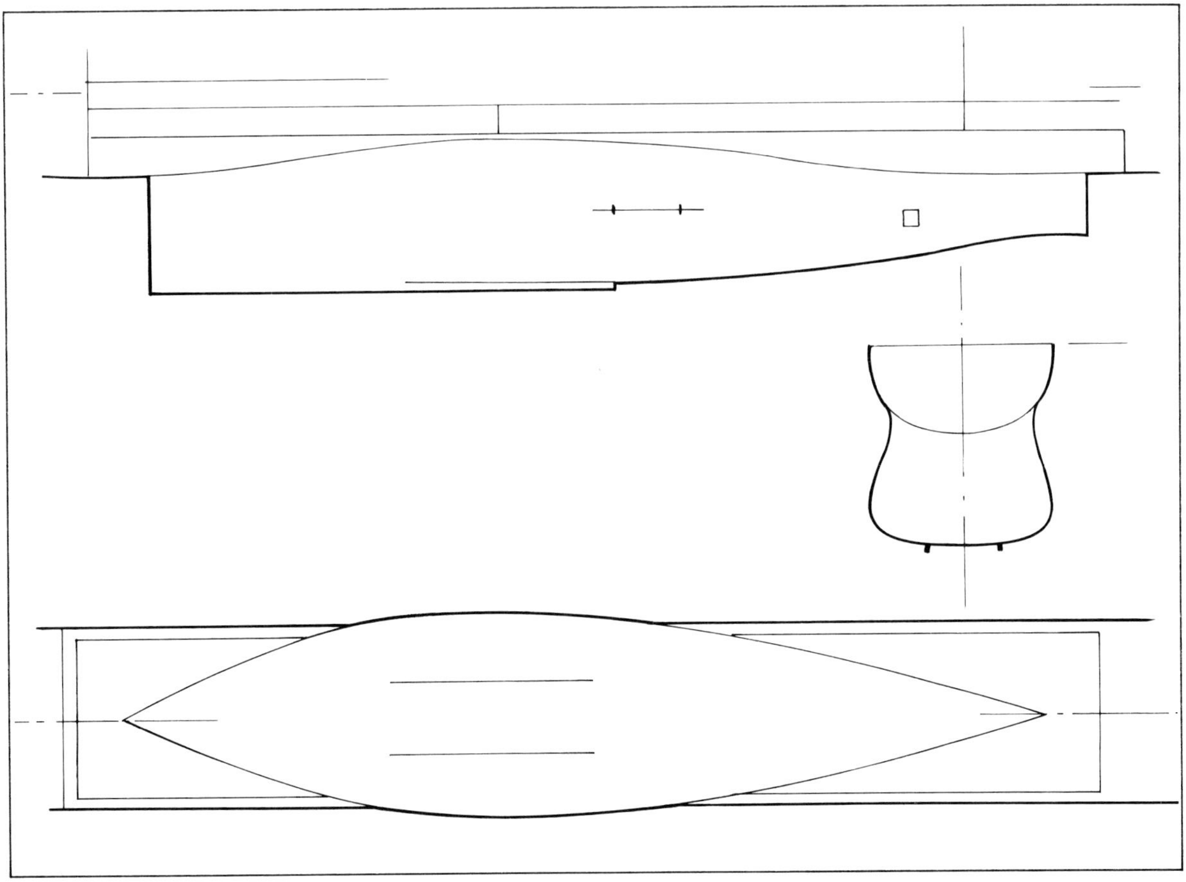

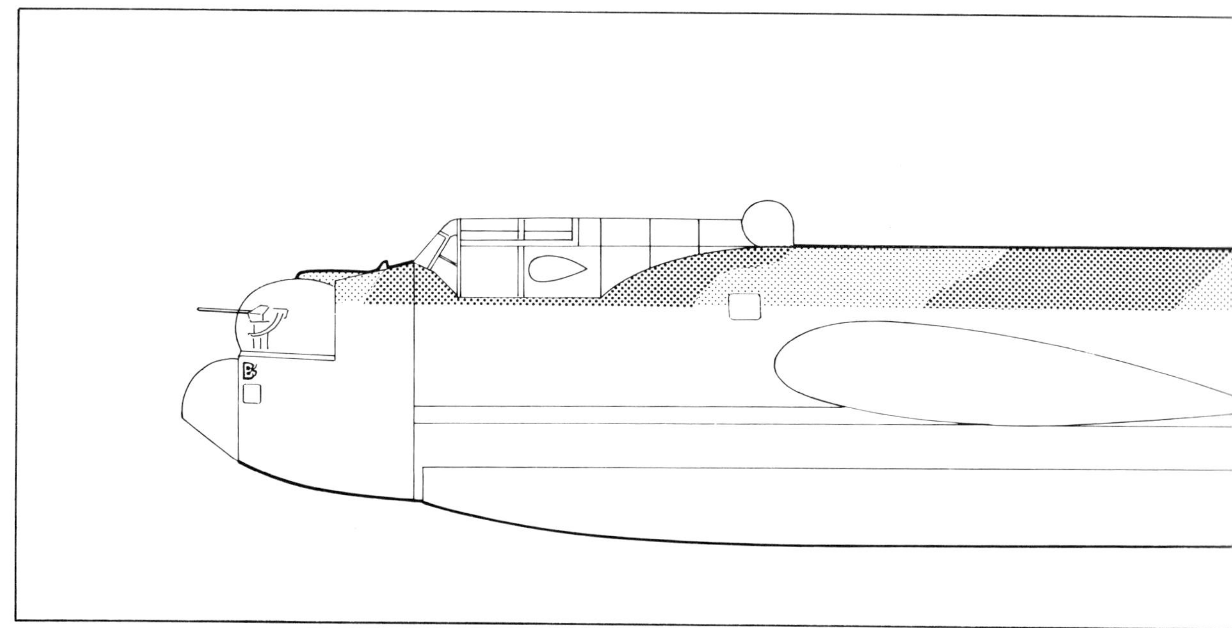

HK 795 of No 149 Squadron at Methwold, 1945, it had yellow G-H bars.

squadron, No 101 at Ludford Magna in Lincolnshire had ABC. This involved the carrying of an eighth crew member who, German speaking, was to broadcast false messages to the *Wilde Sau* and other night fighters to confuse them. Externally, three seven foot aerials were fitted, one under the nose and two on top of the fuselage. Mandril was also an early type of ECM, about one aircraft per squadron being fitted with this as required. A microphone in an engine compartment picked up the noise and this was amplified and broadcast to blank out German radio transmissions.

The problem of rescuing crews whose aircraft had

The Lancaster graveyard at Wroughton. H-X was SW367. H-D, RF325, is the fifth in line.

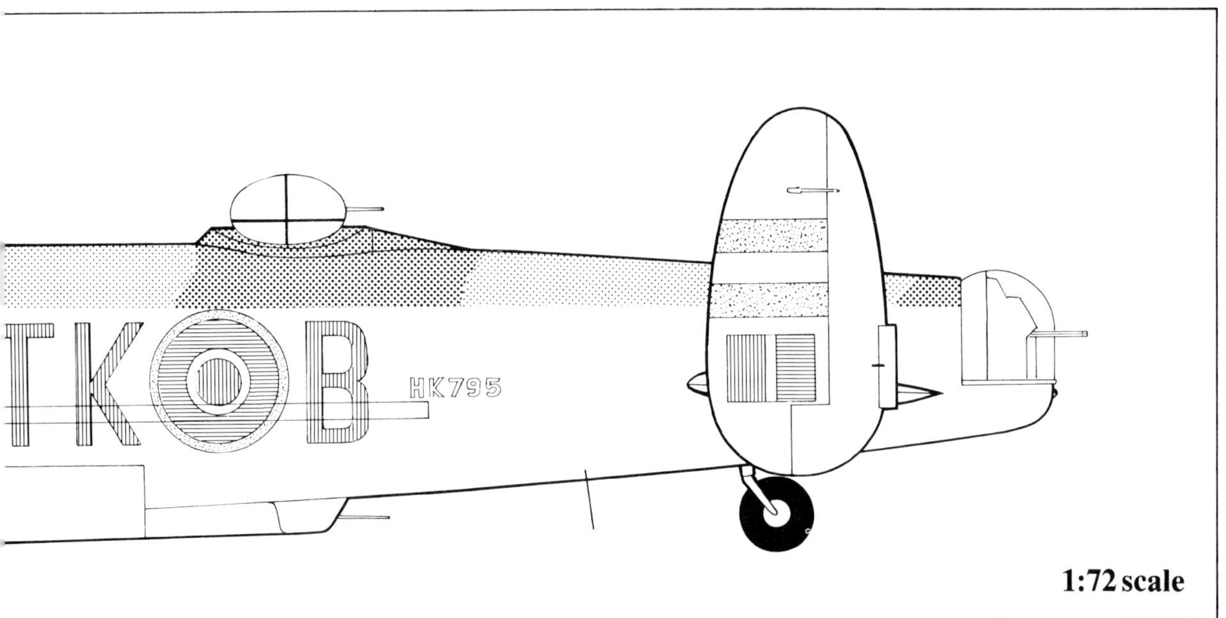

ditched in the sea, either shot up or due to mechanical failure, was a subject which taxed leaders on both sides during World War 2 as it greatly affected morale. Air-sea rescue was a big factor, Lysanders and Spitfires carrying rescue gear, Hudsons carrying Lindholme gear and then being adapted for dropping airborne lifeboats, as was the Warwick. Initially with the Mk I boat, 17 feet 9 inches long, designed by Uffa Fox, this was replaced by the Mk IA, 23 feet 6 inches long and 5 feet 6 inches wide, weighing 17,000 lb and powered by two Britannia 'Middy' 4 hp two-stroke engines. Warwicks first equipped No 280 Squadron based at Strubby, Lincolnshire.

Eventually the Airborne Lifeboat Mk II was developed, this weighing 3,750 lb with a length of 30 feet. This could be carried by the Warwick and many rescues were made, but a more powerful aircraft, with longer range, was sought and the Lancaster was selected. A number of B III Lancasters, mainly new from storage, were sent to Eastleigh, Southampton, where they were converted by Cunliffe Owen Aircraft for air-sea rescue duties and re-designated ASR Mk 3. The Mk II boat was suspended from a single point bomb-slip and dropped by four main parachutes 42 feet in diameter and a single 18 feet diameter retarder 'chute. Powered by a 900 cc Austin four-cylinder marine engine, the boats' beam was 6 feet 6 inches and moulded depth 3 feet 4 inches. Powered range was 600 miles at 4 knots, but this could be extended by use of the sails, fuel tanks holding 50 gallons.

The first drop was made by a No 279 Squadron aircraft from Thornaby on December 10 1945. The Lancaster was RF310, coded RL-A, and the boat was released from 300 feet at 130 knots into wind, using 20° flap, dropping time 32.36 seconds.

The boat was Bermudian Ketch rigged, with triple skinned mahogany hull on rock elm timbers. The two inner skins were layed at about 45° to keel, the top being fore and aft, with proofed calico interleaving between each layer. Planks were about $\frac{1}{8}$ inch thick and 2 inches wide, copper clenched and presenting a smooth carvel finish when complete. Early lifeboats were light blue, as were the sails, with bright orange buoyant canopies fore and aft, the first one dropped was white, as was the underside of the otherwise all slate-grey Lancaster, whilst later ones were all-yellow with a small RAF roundel at the front and black serial number.

GR 3 Lancasters could also carry airborne lifeboats. All had H_2S radomes for ASV radar, with their mid-upper turrets removed and fuselage windows near the tail. Mk IIA airborne lifeboats were introduced in August 1950 but their details are still 'classified'! Both ASR 3 and GR 3 Lancasters were declared obsolete in August 1950, although some were used for training at St Mawgan until October 15 1956 when RF325 was withdrawn and flown to Wroughton in December for scrapping.

A total of 7,377 Lancasters was built including 430 in Canada, as well as spares which would have yielded another 622 airframes. These spares were used by the extensive Lancaster repair organisation to rebuild 3,816 aircraft. In 1943, 55 per cent of all aircraft supplied to the RAF were from the repair organisation, from 1941 to 1945 the average figure was 50 per cent, and the number of employees involved was only 10 per cent of the total in the aircraft industry. We can only praise those who were responsible for founding this efficient organisation!

The wartime development of the Lancaster went hand-in-hand with its equipment, armament, war load, radio, radar and power units, and some details have still to be revealed.

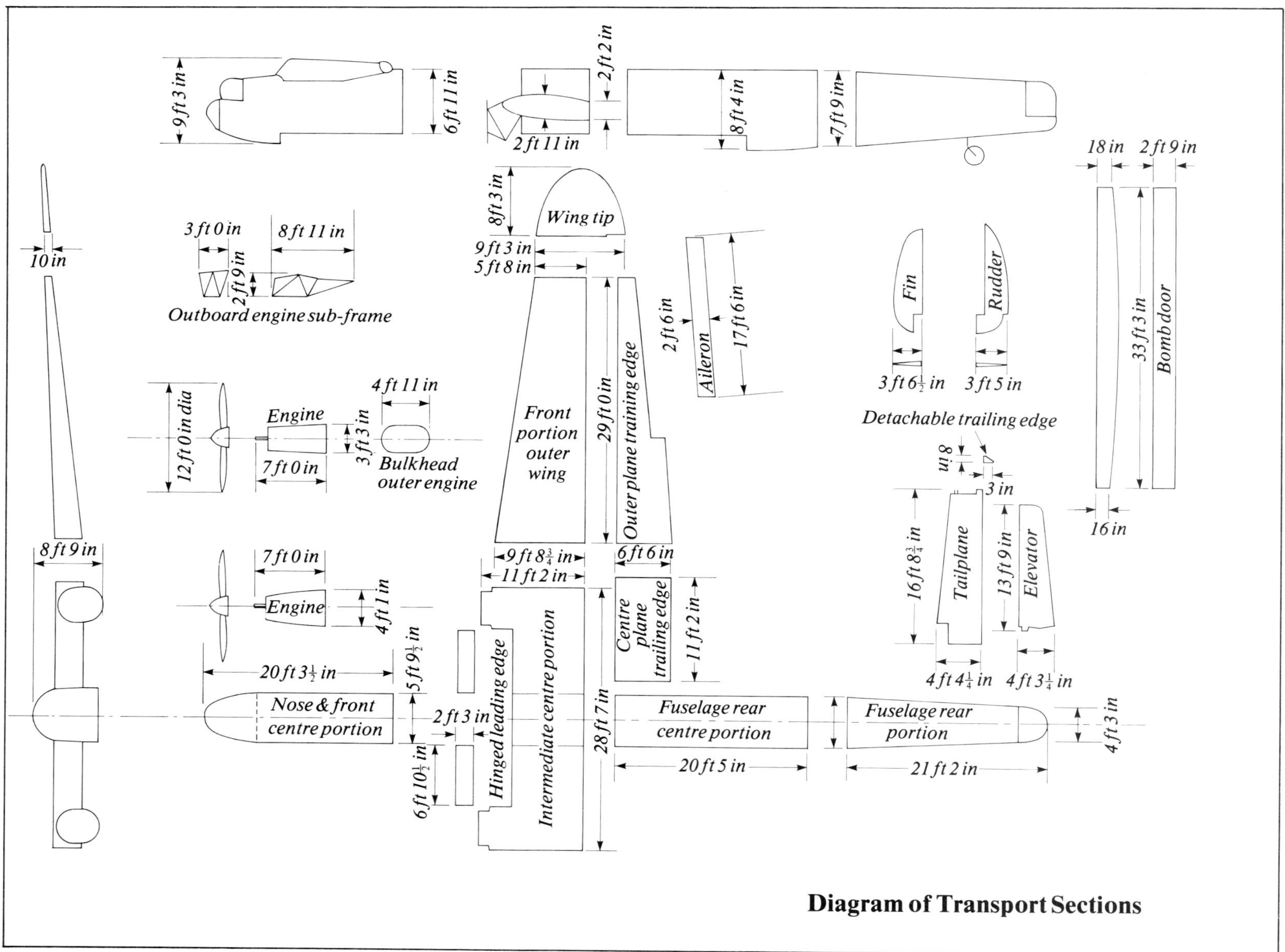

9 ft 3 in
6 ft 11 in
2 ft 2 in
8 ft 4 in
7 ft 9 in
2 ft 11 in
18 in
2 ft 9 in
10 in
3 ft 0 in
8 ft 11 in
2 ft 9 in
Outboard engine sub-frame
8 ft 3 in
Wing tip
9 ft 3 in
5 ft 8 in
2 ft 6 in
Aileron
17 ft 6 in
Fin
Rudder
3 ft 6½ in
3 ft 5 in
Detachable trailing edge
33 ft 3 in
Bomb door
12 ft 0 in dia
Engine
4 ft 11 in
3 ft 3 in
7 ft 0 in
Bulkhead outer engine
Front portion outer wing
29 ft 0 in
Outer plane training edge
8 in
3 in
16 ft 8¾ in
Tailplane
13 ft 9 in
Elevator
16 in
8 ft 9 in
7 ft 0 in
Engine
4 ft 1 in
9 ft 8¾ in
11 ft 2 in
Centre plane trailing edge
11 ft 2 in
4 ft 4¼ in
4 ft 3¼ in
20 ft 3½ in
5 ft 9½ in
Nose & front centre portion
2 ft 3 in
Hinged leading edge
Intermediate centre portion
28 ft 7 in
6 ft 10½ in
6 ft 6 in
Fuselage rear centre portion
Fuselage rear portion
4 ft 3 in
20 ft 5 in
21 ft 2 in
40
Diagram of Transport Sections

Chapter Five

The engine test-beds by Dave Birch

Rolls-Royce's first involvement with the Avro 'heavies' was on December 12 1940 with the arrival at Hucknall of Manchester L7295. The Manchester was earning itself a bad reputation on account of the poor reliability record of its engines, which had a nasty habit of seizing up due to oil circulation problems affecting the main bearings. In an effort to cure the problem, L7295 was sent to Hucknall where its engines were modified to incorporate main bearings containing a certain percentage of lead alloy in their construction instead of the standard silver alloy. An endurance programme was carried out but prematurely concluded by the destruction of the aircraft in a forced landing at Tern Hill in May 1941. The cause of the crash was established as coolant loss from the starboard engine causing seizure and consequent loss of power.

Prior to the arrival of the Manchester at Hucknall, A.V. Roe had begun to redesign the type to accept four Merlin engines. In June 1940 Hucknall began delivery of Merlin XX power plants for Beaufighters. This involved the assembly of engine, mounting, air-intake, radiator, cowlings, etc, into a 'ready to bolt on' unit requiring only the connections of engine controls, fuel and oil lines, etc, at the bulkhead. The availability of these units at this time was a godsend to Avro's and, by November 1940, four Beaufighter power plants had been despatched to Woodford, and the following February four more were sent. The first Lancaster, BT308, made its maiden flight on January 9 1941 and, for a brief period early in 1942, was at Hucknall for tests on flame damping exhaust manifolds.

The first of the Hucknall Lancaster test-beds proper was R5849, which arrived on April 24 1942. This aircraft, a standard production model, was powered by Merlin XXs installed in definitive power plants. These differed from the early Beaufighter type in that they were tailored to the individual engine positions, ie, port outer, port inner, starboard inner and starboard outer, and were not interchangeable. R5849 was immediately employed on a 240-hour endurance programme in which evaluation of such power plant components as exhaust system, radiator, oil cooler, etc, were undertaken over prolonged periods of time. Such development might sound unromantic and unexciting but it was of vital importance. A Lancaster crew member undertaking a sortie deep into enemy territory had good cause to be grateful for the reliability that was a result of such development.

At the termination of the endurance programme,

R5849 was re-engined with four Merlin 28s, thus becoming the prototype Mk III. These engines, built by Packard, were the American version of the Merlin XX and were just beginning to arrive in the UK. It was intended that a similar endurance programme be undertaken with the new engines but, after only 124 hours, the decision was taken to re-engine the outboard

Above *A shot showing the starboard MC-type power plants on Lancaster LM 426. The protruding exhaust shields are particularly evident.*

Below *A starboard-inner Merlin 28 installation in the prototype Lancaster BIII, R5849* (Rolls-Royce Ltd).

positions with the latest idea in power plant design, the circular shaped Universal power plant (UPP). More about that later.

The job of developing the standard Lancaster power plant was entrusted to LM426, a Mk III aircraft delivered in December 1943. With the rapid build up of service experience of the Lanc power plant came the inevitable improvements brought about by prolonged utilisation under conditions that could not be simulated by a limited period of development flying, however intense. Coupled with this were the improvements initiated by the Installation Design Department at Hucknall, who, in their efforts to improve reliability, were coming up with new designs, new materials and new methods of construction. In order to differentiate between the varying standards of power plant a simple identification system was devised. The Merlin power plants were given a two-letter code beginning with M, the first being type MA and installed in the early Lancaster 1s and IIIs. Next came the MB which featured various modifications including side panels made in two sections (the split being immediately behind the exhaust shroud), a flexibly mounted header tank with a quick release filler cap, and an emergency hot air system (to prevent the carburettor from icing up) that obtained its air from behind the radiators instead of from within the engine cowling itself. The final single-stage Merlin power plant to go into production was the MC which was interchangeable with the MA and MB. It is difficult visually to identify the first two types from one another but the problem does not arise with the MC. The most notable external features are the large open-ended flame damping ducts which conceal the exhaust fishtails. This duct was bolted on to the engine itself whereas on previous designs it had been fastened to the cowling, whereupon it had been the source of many maintenance problems, chiefly caused by vibration. The new duct protruded from the cowling to a far greater extent than on the MA and MB types. Another major change was the placing of the radiator and oil cooler in series instead of side by side. This meant that air passed through the radiator and then through the oil cooler which was directly behind it, the latter being of the same shape and frontal area of the former but of less volume.

To meet the needs of Transport Command the MB and MC power plants were modified slightly and given the prefix letter T. The differences, in the main, concerned the exhaust system whereby the redundancy of flame damping requirements meant a change to circular outlet exhaust stubs instead of fishtails. The TMB and TMC types were fitted to the York and Lancastrian. These aircraft were powered by the standard Merlin 24 or its modified counterpart, the T 24/2. For the Trans-Canada Airlines Lancastrians, an afterheater was incorporated between the supercharger and induction manifold in order to raise the charge (fuel-air mixture) temperature. This was found to be necessary because of the unique operating conditions whereby these aircraft flew for many hours cruising at low boost pressures. In order to prevent the sparking plugs from leading-up, the charge leaving the supercharger had to be heated up to a degree compatible with that obtained by high boosts. These engines became the T 24/4. The development of the Merlin 24 and its transport variants was entrusted to LM426, ND340 and PP779. With the development of the T 24/4 engine a number of TCA Lancastrians were sent to Hucknall for conversion during the winter of 1945-46; they were CF-CMX, CMY, CMZ and CNA, the latter three later gracing the British register as G-AKDP, DR and DS.

Back in June 1941, Rolls-Royce proposed a five-engined Lancaster. Basically, it featured a single-speed Merlin (45 or 46) installed within the fuselage and driving a huge slave supercharger that supplied air, via ducting, to the blowers of the four wing-mounted engines, providing in effect, two-stage supercharging. This scheme, though relatively simple, had its drawbacks, not the least of which was what happened when an engine had to be shut down, either for mechanical reasons or by the puncturing of the ducting through enemy action. On the positive side it was estimated that, at an all-up weight of 60,000 lb, the ceiling of the Lancaster would be 44,000 feet, which by any reckoning was fantastic. In view of this remarkable performance, the effect of replacing the standard engines with the new two-stage supercharged Merlin 60 was not considered, the installation of such engines being deemed a considerable complication at that stage even though it would have been beneficial to performance. However, like a thousand and one other projects during the war, this one also died a natural death and never got any further than the drawing board. Almost two years later, in a complete reversal of earlier policy it was decided to install the two-stage Merlin instead, although the end result would not be as spectacular as the original proposal. The cowlings of the standard Lancaster power plants all differed in some respect from each other. This was because the auxiliaries, eg, engine-driven accessories such as the hydraulic pump, were mounted on the engine itself. Another reason was that the bulkhead profiles were not identical. By making the engine bulkheads circular and of a common diameter and mounting the accessories either on the bulkhead or behind it, a standardised power plant was achieved. Furthermore, if the bulkhead diameter was made sufficient in the first place then larger and more powerful engines could be installed without any modification to the aircraft.

It was decided that the powerful Merlin 65 engine should be installed in the first UPP installation. These engines had two-stage supercharging as opposed to the Merlin XX series' single stage and were capable of delivering 1,705 hp against the Merlin 28s 1,460 hp. The first flight of R5849 with Merlin 28s inboard and Merlin 65s outboard took place on May 6 1943. Its development career was, however, short lived. On June 11 whilst on the approach to Hucknall at the end of a routine flight, there was an explosion in the region of the port wheel bay followed by fire. The aircraft was landed

An early post-war picture of Lancaster VI DV170 powered by four Merlin 102s in Tudor power plants (Rolls Royce Ltd).

safely but, in the ensuing conflagration, R5849 was totally destroyed.

In order to continue the flight development of the Universal power plant with the minimum of delay, Lancaster DV170, which had been earmarked for Merlin 28 development, was converted to the same configuration as the late R5849 and as such was flown in late August 1943. After 116 hours flying the inboard engines were changed to Merlin 38s (the Packard version of the Merlin 22) and the outboards were fitted with the Merlin 85. The latter engine, which was the Merlin 65 fitted with an auxiliary gearbox drive, had been chosen for the high flying Lancaster IV project which, in the event became the Lincoln. DV170 first took this combination into the air on November 3 1943 and, five weeks later, Lancaster DV199 took to the air with four UPPs installed, thus becoming the prototype Mk VI. This machine featured Merlin 65s inboard and 85s outboard. Over the following years these two aircraft were to be fully employed on the flight development of the Universal power plant, not only for military use but also for such civil ventures as the Tudor and DC-4M.

When DV199 arrived at Hucknall it was a standard Mk III aircraft equipped with Merlin 28s and the opportunity was taken to undertake a complete performance investigation. This included establishing the maximum speed at the all-up weight of 60,000 lb so that a comparison could be made of any improvement obtained by the installation of the two-stage engines. It

was established that, in standard condition, the top speed of DV199 was 257 mph at 19,000 feet with the Merlin 28s operating at +9 psi boost. As a Mk VI, with engines operating at +18 psi boost, the top speed had risen to $304\frac{1}{2}$ mph at 18,000 feet, an improvement of 47 mph.

A number of Lancaster IIIs were converted to VIs by Rolls-Royce at Hucknall for use by Bomber Command. A total of seven conversions were undertaken, commencing November 1943, and five of them were issued to squadrons based at Wyton, 635 Squadron receiving them all at one time or another. They were: JB713, JB675, ND418, ND479, ND558, ND673 and ND784. Two of these, JB675 and ND558, eventually returned to Hucknall and were employed on UPP development along with DV170 and DV199, whilst ND784 eventually became the Armstrong Siddeley Mamba flying test-bed. The prototype TCA Lancaster, CF-CMS, was also at Hucknall where it was fitted with Merlin T 85s in TMH power plants (the Lancaster VIs had MH type). Not to be outdone, BOAC sent its civil Lancaster G-AGJI to have Merlin 102s installed in similar fashion to gain engine handling experience in readiness for the Tudor airliner.

One Hucknall Lanc which never left the ground was EE134, a veteran of 99 ops with 49 and 619 Squadrons. The inboard engine installations were converted to UPPs and employed on fire prevention investigation. During these tests the engine would be run up to high

Lancaster VI DV199 with four Merlin 85s installed in Universal power plants (Rolls-Royce Ltd).

Above *TCA Lancaster CF-CMS at Hucknall (prior to conversion) with standard Merlin 38s installed* (Rolls-Royce Ltd).

Below *CF-CMS after conversion with Merlin T85 engines installed in Universal power plants* (Rolls-Royce Ltd).

Below *A close-up of the Dart installation in the nose of NG465 showing the spray grid structure* (Rolls-Royce Ltd).

rpm, after which petrol was pumped into the nacelle, so simulating a serious fuel leak. The resultant conflagration would be assisted by the slipstream of a revving Lancaster positioned immediately in front of EE134. With the activation of the fire detection and extinguisher systems, evaluation was made of their effectiveness.

The final development Lancaster to arrive at Hucknall was NG465, in August 1946. A conversion was undertaken whereby a Dart turboprop was installed in the nose following which the first flight of this historic turbine took place on October 10 1947. To enable investigation into icing conditions a water spray grid was positioned in front of the engine supported by a massive tubular structure. The grid's nozzles sprayed fine jets of water which, in the cold atmosphere, would congeal as

Lancaster EE134, Semper en Excretia, *well and truly ablaze during a test run to evaluate the fire detection and extinguisher systems* (Rolls-Royce Ltd).

ice upon the air intake, spinner and oil cooler. When a sufficient amount of ice had built up, the de-icing equipment was switched on and its effect evaluated. As the ice loosened its grip large chunks were ingested by the engine, which would then be closely examined to see what effect the passage of such solid objects through it would have. After 800 hours of development flying, the career of NG465 came to an abrupt end in a forced landing on Holinwell golf course just north of Hucknall on January 22 1954. This accident brought to a close the Lancaster era at Hucknall, to be followed a year later by the last of the Lancastrians.

1945 saw the arrival of a Lancastrian at the Rolls-Royce Flight Test Establishment and two of them were to play a significant part in the Nene gas turbine development programme. The Lancastrian was the perfect vehicle for this type of work, for a variety of reasons. Being a four-engined aircraft it meant that two positions could be converted to take the jets, thus enabling each flight to produce twice as much development flying time as the alternative of, say, mounting the test engine in the rear fuselage or bomb bay. The outboard positions were chosen so that the jet efflux would not impinge upon the tail fins, though some aileron span was sacrificed. The retention of proven piston engines in the inboard positions meant that, in the event of failure of the jets, the aircraft could return to base safely. Employing a large aircraft for this type of work also meant that a generous fuel tankage was available, both to feed the thirsty jets and to provide flights of greater endurance than was previously possible. Finally, being a passenger-carrying aircraft, the Lancastrian offered comfortable accommodation for a greater number of flight test engineers and their equipment.

PD167 was the first to arrive in August. The following month its serial was changed to VH737 by which time it had been placed in storage at Church Broughton, Derbyshire; Rolls-Royce's base for testing its gas turbine powered aircraft at that time. In April 1946 it returned to Hucknall and work commenced on converting its outboard positions to take the Nene engine. By January 1947 the conversion was complete and the 1090 flight was undertaken on the 17th. In April, VH737 was despatched to RAE Farnborough and, on its return four months later, was fitted with a water spray grid on the port-outer installation to simulate icing conditions. In November 1948 the inboard Merlin 24s were replaced by Merlin 621s in Tudor power plants, the first flight as such taking place on the last day of February 1949. The aircraft then pursued a lengthy test programme until it was finally pensioned off in March 1952 after 406 flying hours.

Perhaps the most famous of all Lancastrian flying test-beds was VH742, which was delivered to Hucknall in October 1945. Immediately on arrival, it underwent conversion to Nenes in the manner prescribed for VH737 and took to the air for the first time on August 14 1946. By September it had flown a total of 28 hours and, on the 10th, was flown to Radlett for exhibition at the SBAC show. In a sense this was the world's first airliner in as much as, prior to its arrival, the only people who had flown in a jet aircraft were test pilots and their engineers and Service pilots. Now, with its inward facing row of seats VH742 played host to various dignitaries and, in particular, to the aviation press who went into raptures at the experience. September 19 1946 was a busy day for the Rolls-Royce public relations department when VH742 made three flights carrying correspondents from *Flight, Aeroplane and Aeronautics* and such dailies as the *Express, Graphic* and *Herald*, not to mention representatives from A. V. Roe and the Ministry of Supply. The following week *Flight* reported 'Flying in the Lancastrian, using only its two Nenes, is a memorable experience, and one immediately feels like repeating to everyone "you must try it". It is no exaggeration to say that any airline which could now introduce an all jet service would revolutionise air

Above *VH742 the first of two Nene Lancastrians. The inboard Merlins are feathered in this picture. All told, eight Lancastrians were converted to take jets in their outboard positions* (Rolls-Royce Ltd).

Below *VH737, the second Nene Lancastrian, showing the water-spray grid fitted for anti-icing investigation* (Rolls-Royce Ltd).

Above *A view of the Avon installation in Lancastrian VM732* (Rolls-Royce Ltd).

transport and be the talk of the world. It is not just a case of being noiseless, but even more important, it is vibrationless. The appeal of gliding with its silent, graceful motion and the gentle swish of the air, is immediately understandable'.

A total of 639 hours was flown by VH742 with Nenes installed, the final flight being on August 4 1949. It was then passed on to the workshops for conversion to Tay engines, work continuing on a low priority until October when the project was cancelled. The aircraft was then stored for a year after which it was dismantled and despatched to the Proof and Experimental Establishment at Shoeburyness.

The Lancastrian was also well suited to test the AJ65 Avon engine. This engine was the company's first gas turbine with an axial compressor; the previous designs, Derwent, Nene and Tay all having a centrifugal compressor. Two such conversions were undertaken at Hucknall; the first, VM732 after being used initially on noise abatement tests, these being chiefly concerned with the evaluation of the Tudor and DC-4M North Star exhaust systems. Following the conversion, the Avon took to the air for the first time on August 15 1948 and, during the next 13 months, a total of 273 hours were flown by VM732 on its development by which time it had been joined by a second Lancastrian conversion, VL970, upon which development was now concentrated. The second Avon flying test-bed differed from the first in that the inboard Merlin T 24s were replaced by Merlin 623 engines in Tudor power plants. The port Avon installation also featured a water spray grid. VL970 first flew as such on June 16 1949. This particular aircraft was by far the most extensively used Lancastrian at Hucknall and, in all, spent nearly six years testing Avon engines up to the RA 7. Unhappily its career ended in tragedy when on March 29 1955, after 666 flying hours, it was totally destroyed in a crash at Hucknall, killing all four crew.

In order to gain as much experience as possible with Tudor power plants under actual operating conditions, Lancastrian VM728 was converted to take Merlin 600s, operating at +25 lb boost with water methanol injection, on the inboard positions, and on the outboard Merlin 641s, which were 621s with a higher compression ratio. This aircraft undertook an endurance programme which entailed the accumulation of 1,000 flying hours, and this it achieved between September 1947 and June 1948, often flying for more than ten hours a day.

In the mid-1940s, Rolls-Royce designed a large turboprop of 3,500 shp called the Clyde and the Lancastrian was chosen as its test vehicle. Just after the arrival at Hucknall of the two aircraft chosen for conversion, in June 1947, the whole project was

dropped. The company's increasing involvement with the production and development of the Derwent, Nene, Dart and Avon, not to mention the Merlin and Griffon, had given the Clyde a low priority, though it did in fact fly later in a Westland Wyvern. The two Lancastrians, VM704 and VM733, were given other work, the latter being employed on comparison tests with Rotol and de Havilland airscrews. This aircraft eventually found its way to Armstrong Siddeley's for Sapphire development. For VM704 much greater things were destined. A complete conversion was undertaken whereby the outboard engines were replaced by Merlin 623s in Tudor power plants and the inboards with the Griffon 57 in Shackleton nacelles. The first flight of this hybrid configuration was made on October 19 1948, and tests continued until May 1952, by which time almost 500 hours had been accumulated. Merlin 625 and 641s were also installed in the outboard positions at various times.

Although Rolls-Royce were to remain unchallenged as the most prolific converter of the Lancaster and Lancastrian, other companies were equally enthusiastic in employing Avro's bomber as a vehicle for flight-testing their engines. Indeed, the first turbine conversion was flown some three years before that of Rolls-Royce. In 1937, the Metropolitan-Vickers company, in co-operation with the RAE, began development of a gas turbine engine and, right from the start, it was decided to employ an axial compressor as opposed to the centrifugal type featured in the Whittle designs. After running a couple of experimental units on the bench, a finalised design known as the F 1 was constructed in 1940, producing around 2,600 lb of thrust. After further modifications the F 2 emerged and, eventually, from this, came a flight test engine, F 2 No 3 derated to give 1,800 lb thrust. This unit was installed by Armstrong Whitworth in the rear fuselage of the prototype Lancaster BT308, making its first flight from Baginton on June 29 1943. This aircraft was replaced the following year by Lancaster LL735 with an identical conversion; this machine being the sole Lancaster II used as a flying test-bed. The ultimate version of this engine was the F 2/4 Beryl, first of the precious stones range of engines, and this too was to be installed in the tail of LL735. The Beryl was quite advanced for its day and featured a ten stage compressor and annular combustion chamber. Its only other Lancaster installation was in mock-up form, by Air Service

Above Lancastrian VM728 fitted with Merlin 600s inboard and Merlin 641s outboard. Between September 1947 and June 1948 over 1,000 hours of endurance flying were achieved (Rolls-Royce Ltd).

Below Half of VM704's total of 8,420 horsepower is shown in this picture. Griffon 57 engines are installed inboard, in Shackleton power plants, driving contra-rotating propellers. The outer installations are Merlin 623s in Tudor power plants (Rolls-Royce Ltd).

Training in the late 1940s. The only other aeronautical application of the Beryl was its installation in a Meteor 4 and the Saunders-Roe SR A1 flying boat fighter prototypes.

Armstrong Siddeley also entered the gas turbine scene at an early stage when, in 1942, they received a contract to produce an axial jet, which emerged the following year as the ASX of 2,600 lb thrust. Air Service Training at Hamble were given the task of installing the engine in the bomb bay of Lancaster VI ND784 and, as such, the first flight was made in June of 1945. Flight tests totalled 48 hours by which time it had been decided to concentrate on the turbo-prop version, the ASP, which had made its initial run in March 1945. Lancaster TW911 was converted to take two of these engines, known by then as the Python, in the outboard positions. These engines each weighed twice as much as the Merlins that they replaced and, as originally installed, were

Top *Running up Pythons in Lancaster TW911.*

Above *A Shackleton? No, a head-on view of the Python-powered Lancaster TW9118.*

Below *The Python-powered Lancaster TW911, with air intakes cut back by 4 feet 9 inches.*

shrouded by long chord nacelles wherein the air intake was positioned immediately behind the spinner. After a short period of flying, which commenced on January 3 1949, the intake was repositioned much further back and nearer the wing leading edge in order to serve more favourably the reverse flow conditions which were a feature of this engine. Equipped with contra-rotating props and delivering 3,560 ehp, the Python was destined to have a limited career and served only in the Westland Wyvern naval strike aircraft.

With the termination of the ASX project, ND784 was sent to AST for its second conversion, this time to take a turbo-prop. A Mamba 2 was installed in the nose and the first flight made on October 14 1947, just four days after the maiden flight of its competitor, the Rolls-Royce Dart. This 850 shp engine, the second of the Reptile class, was to achieve success only as a twin unit installed in the Fairey Gannet. A fresh approach to the flight testing of the Mamba was undertaken with the conversion of a second aircraft, Lancaster SW342, which differed from the original in having a water spray grid fitted to enable icing trials to be carried out. The width of the structure was much narrower than that of the Dart installation on NG465 which meant that the propeller had to be of a much smaller diameter than standard, the blades being of extremely wide chord. This machine took to the air in June 1949. In 1951, a sixth engine was added in a tail installation similar to that of the early Metra-Vick test-beds. The new engine, an Adder of 1,050 lb thrust, was a pure jet version of the Mamba and was intended as a short life unit to power target aircraft. It had originally been flown in the Pika, the predecessor of the Jindivik radio controlled target. By November 1952, it had been replaced by the long life version, the Viper. The first of its type to fly in SW342 was the Viper 3 rated at 1,640 lb thrust and, later, a Viper 7R was installed for reheat experiments. The Viper entered full production and became the most successful of the Armstrong Siddeley turbines, remaining in production at the time of writing.

When Metropolitan-Vickers terminated all work on gas turbines in 1948, they had just begun to test their latest design, the F 9. A development of the Beryl, it featured a 13-stage compressor and delivered over 7,000 lb of thrust. All work on the F 9 was taken over by Armstrong Siddeley who, in respect for Metro-Vick, retained the name chosen for the engine—Sapphire. The Sapphire was a particularly good engine and was later the subject of a licence agreement with the Wright Corporation in America who produced it as the J 65. Its first flight, however, was made in the outboard positions of Lancastrian VM733 on January 19 1950. During its long career the Sapphire was produced and supported under five company flags; Metropolitan-Vickers, Armstrong Siddeley, Wright, Bristol Siddeley and Rolls-Royce.

The de Havilland company initiated its gas turbine experience early in 1941 when they began the design of not only a new engine but also a new aircraft to receive it. The engine was the 3,000 lb thrust H 1 Goblin and the

ASX installed in the bomb bay of Lancaster VI ND784 and tested from Bruntingthorpe (Rolls-Royce Ltd).

aircraft the Vampire. An enlarged version of the Goblin was the H 2 Ghost, initially rated at 4,000 lb thrust but put into production at almost 5,000 lb. Although first flown in a Vampire, de Havilland adopted the Rolls-Royce approach and converted a couple of Lancastrians to take Ghosts in the outboard nacelles, the first of these, VM703 making its initial flight on July 24 1947. The early Ghost engines had bifurcated air intakes to suit the Vampire/Venom installations but, for the Comet airliner, a conventional central entry intake was employed. As thus it was known as the Ghost 50 and it was these units that were installed in the Lancastrians. The first conversion was also employed in investigations into rocket assisted take-off and, for these tests, a couple of German Walter 109-500 rocket motors were slung externally beneath the fuselage. The second conversion, VM729, was mainly employed on Ghost certification and development for the Comet. Between them these two aircraft achieved approximately 850 flying hours.

In 1949 the Swedish company STAL (Svenska

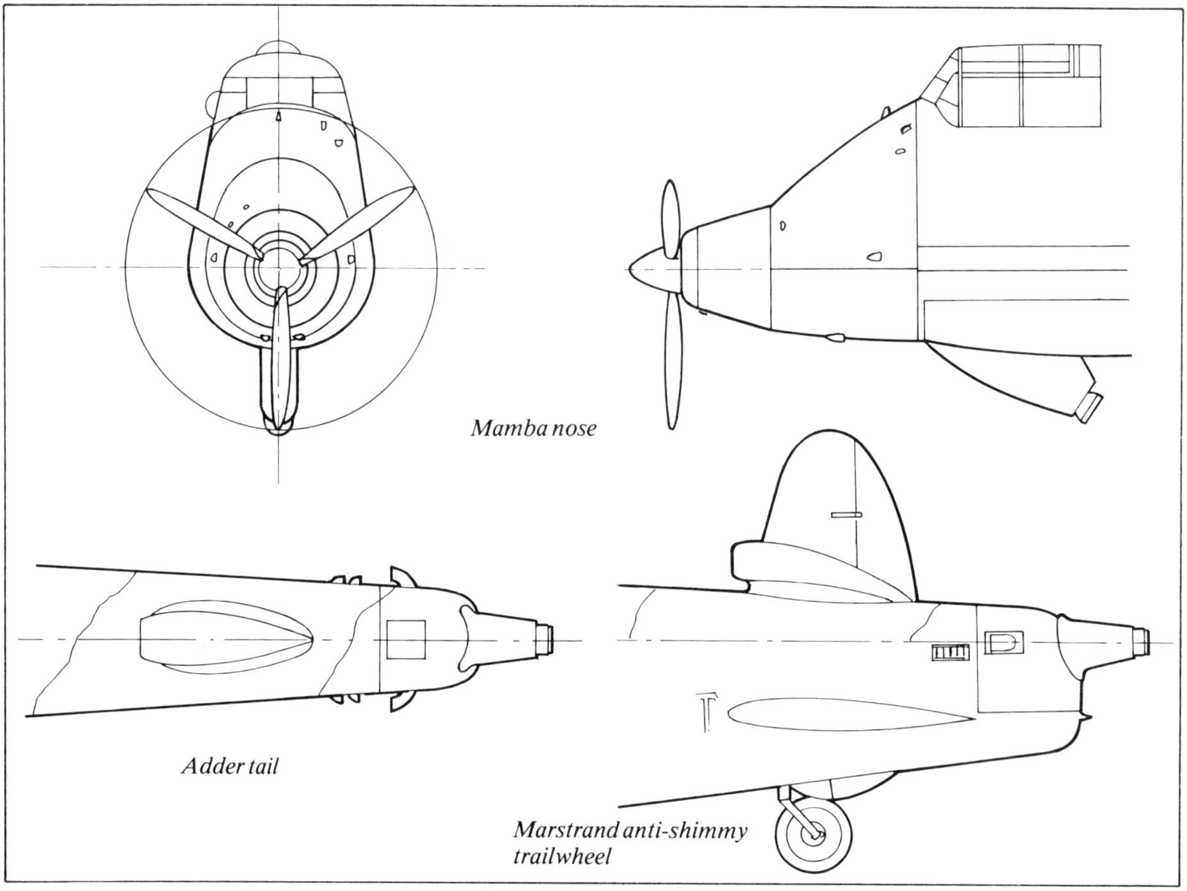

Mamba nose

Adder tail

*Marstrand anti-shimmy
trailwheel*

Below *The Swedish test-bed Lanc Tp18 (ex-RA805) fitted with Stal Dovern. White spinner, grey top, remainder black.*

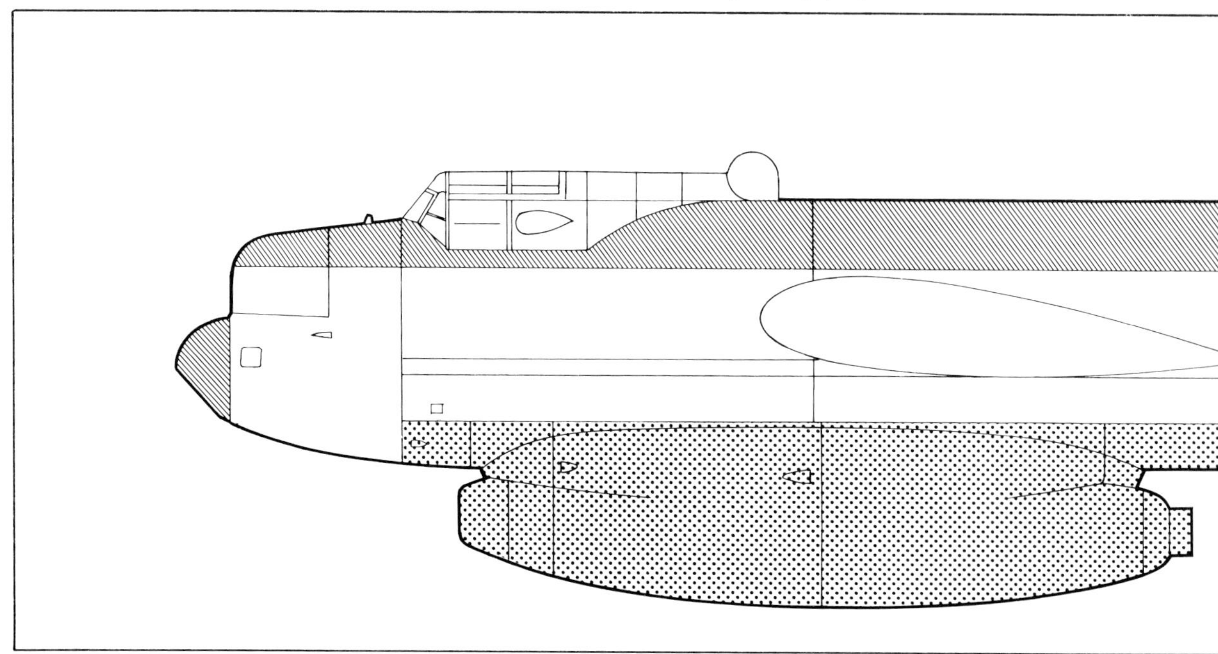

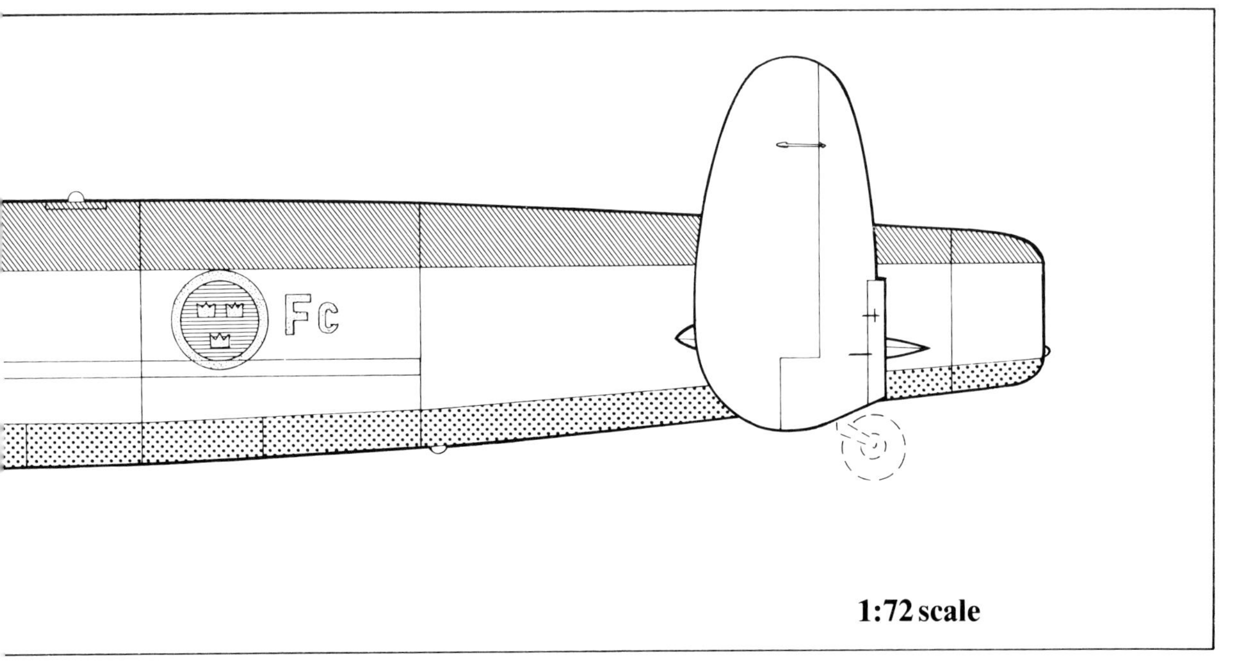

Above *A close-up of Air Service Training's Dovern pod opened up.*

Above *This Lancastrian, VM703, coded R, was used by De Havilland for testing their Ghost turbojet. Re-heat was also tested on this aircraft* (British Aerospace).

Below right *The Sapphire-powered Lancastrian VM733.*

Below left *A Mamba installation in Lancaster SW 342 showing the spray-grid and wide-chord, small-diameter propeller.*

Below *Lancaster SW342—Mamba in nose, Adder in tail.*

Turbinfabriks AB Ljungström), in conjunction with Svenska Flygmotor, began running an axial jet of their own design named the Dovern. It was rated at 7,275 lb thrust and featured a nine-stage compressor. To flight-test the engine, a surplus Lancaster from the Argentine contract (RA805) was delivered to AST at Hamble where an under-the-fuselage installation was completed and test-flown for the first time on April 24 1951. The acceptance flights were achieved with a mock-up engine installed, the real thing being fitted in Sweden. The aircraft bore the serial 80001 and was operated by Kungl Flygfor Naltningon at Malmslatt. With the termination of the Dovern project, 80001 was converted for a second time; to air-test the Ghost reheat engine intended for the Saab J29F fighter.

And finally Canada, where the Avro concern converted a Lancaster X, FM209, to take two Orenda axial jets in the outboard positions. The 6,000 lb thrust Orenda was Avro Canada's second excursion into the gas turbine field, the first being the smaller Chinook, some two years previously, which did not fly. FM209 took to the air for the first time on July 13 1950, and enjoyed a lengthy career until destroyed by fire in 1956.

The following is a list of the types of engines flown in the Lancaster and Lancastrian and, where known, the individual aircraft and date of the first flight.

Rolls-Royce

Merlin XX	Lancaster	BT308	9.1.41
Merlin 22	Lancaster		
Merlin 24	Lancaster		
Merlin T 24	Lancaster	G-AGJI	28.9.44
Merlin 28	Lancaster	R5849	26.9.42
Merlin 38	Lancaster		
Merlin 65	Lancaster	R5849	11.5.43
Merlin 85	Lancaster	DV170	3.11.43
Merlin T 85	Lancaster	CF-CMS	31.12.44
Merlin 100	Lancaster	DV199	12.5.44
Merlin 102	Lancaster	JB675	15.5.45
Merlin 150	Lancaster	JB675	28.2.46
Merlin 224	Lancaster		
Merlin 500	Lancastrian		
Merlin 600	Lancastrian	VM728	29.8.47
Merlin 620	Lancaster	JB675	6.12.46
Merlin 621	Lancaster	JB675	6.12.46
Merlin 623	Lancastrian	VM728	9.8.48
Merlin 625	Lancastrian	VM704	6.2.50
Merlin 630	Lancaster	JB675	4.3.47
Merlin 640	Lancaster	JB675	1.7.47
Merlin 641	Lancaster	JB675	5.5.47

Three other Merlin types, known only by their ratings, were flown for the first time in a Lancaster, DV199, on 24.2.45. They were RM 11 SM, RM 14 SM and RM 16 SM.

Griffon 57	Lancastrian	VM704	19.10.48
Nene RN 1	Lancastrian	VH742	14.8.46
Nene RN 2	Lancastrian		
Avon RA 2	Lancastrian	VM732	15.8.48
Avon RA 3	Lancastrian	VL970	27.10.49
Avon RA 7	Lancastrian	VL970	
Avon 502	Lancastrian	VL970	
Dart RDa 1	Lancaster	NG465	10.10.47
Dart RDa 3	Lancaster	NG465	
Dart RDa 4	Lancaster	NG465	49

Bristol

Hercules VI	Lancaster	DT810	21.12.41
Hercules XVI	Lancaster		

Armstrong-Siddeley

ASX	Lancaster	ND784	6.45
Mamba ASMa 2	Lancaster	ND784	14.10.47
Python ASP 1	Lancaster	TW911	3.1.49
Adder	Lancaster	SW342	51
Viper ASV 3	Lancaster	SW342	11.52
Viper ASV 7R	Lancaster	SW342	
Sapphire ASSa2	Lancastrian	VM733	19.1.50
Sapphire ASSa3	Lancastrian	VM733	11.50

No doubt other marks of Mamba and Sapphire were flown in SW342 and VM733 but no details have come to light.

de Havilland

Ghost D Gt 50	Lancastrian	VM703	24.7.47

Avro Canada

Orenda	Lancastrian	FM209	13.7.50

STAL

Dovern	Lancaster	80001	51

Walter

109-500	Lancastrian	VM703	

Chapter Six

Victory in Europe and after

Although hostilities ended in Europe in May 1945, the day of the Lancaster was not over, for some 74,000 prisoners of war were air-lifted home from Germany. A month earlier, these same Lancasters, in over 3,000 sorties, dropped 6,685 tons of supplies, food and clothes to the starving Dutch in Rotterdam and other towns in western Holland, in Operation 'Manna' during the first week of May. The Lancs were hastily equipped to carry soldiers, sailors and airmen, some of whom had been prisoners for five years. No-one would have suggested that it was a comfortable journey, crowded together in the noisy rear fuselage, but who cared!?

Tours were flown over bomb-damaged German targets to show ground-crews what they had helped to achieve with their long, arduous hours of painstaking maintenance before getting down to the task of finishing the war in the Pacific theatre. It had been planned to equip 'Tiger' force with the higher powered and longer ranged Lincoln but it was felt to be a mistake to upset production lines geared to turning out Lancasters at rates up to 400 per month.

Experiments with saddle tanks had been made on two Lancasters to increase their fuel capacity by 1,200 gallons. Long-range flights experimenting with new navigation aids had been carried out by the Central Navigation School from Shawbury using a Wellington and a Stirling with Lancaster PD328, later 'Aries', taking over in 1944. Tropical development using larger radiators had also taken place so, from the end of 1944, plans to equip three groups, each with ten squadrons, together with long-range escort fighters, went ahead.

New Lancasters from the production lines of Vickers Armstrong and Armstrong Whitworth were flown to Belfast for conversion to Far East standard by Short Bros. Mk 1, III and VII Lancasters were to be modified, all having the higher powered Mk 24 series Merlin, with mid-upper turrets removed to compensate for a 400-gallon long-range tank fitted in the bomb-bay, and American radios installed (SCR-522) compatible with communications equipment already used in the Pacific war. With white upper surfaces but still black underneath, although large white serials appeared under the wings, several squadrons, among them nos 35, 70, 104, 115, 138 and 207, were equipped but then the end came—B-29s flying from the Marianas dropped single atomic bombs on Hiroshima and Nagasaki during the first week of August, and the war was over!

The first squadron for 'Tiger' force was not scheduled to leave for Okinawa, via the Azores and Canada, until November, so they were no longer needed, Bomber Command finished the war with 55 squadrons equipped with 1,375 Lancasters and the Lincoln was about to be issued to No 57 Squadron (three were received before the end of August), so this establishment had to be quickly run down to peace time strength. Lines of Lancasters awaiting scrapping were visible at Wroughton while many were placed in store pending a decision on their fate.

Canadian built Lancasters, 100 of which had been delivered, had been flown back from Valley and Melton Mowbray since 1944 as they were also earmarked for use in the Pacific. Victory Aircraft produced 430 Lancasters and the last were not withdrawn from service until April 1 1964, specialised versions being developed for post-war service, and some were used experimentally. Of 230 Lancasters used by the RCAF, 72 were converted as Mk 10MR (Maritime Reconnaissance) later 10MP (Maritime Patrol), ten became 10P, serving with No 408

A Lancaster B1 with a long-range 'saddle' tank (Roy Cross).

No 300 (Masovian) Squadron flying from Faldingworth in 1946. BH-Z, S and B (PB705) from front to rear.

Squadron at Rockcliffe for photo-reconnaissance, two having radio altimeters for a mapping survey of northern Canada, ten were converted for Air-Sea Rescue in 1949 as Mk 10SR, three became Mk 10N navigation trainers, five were winterised for Mk 10BR bomber reconnaissance whilst a further batch became Mk 10AR for aerial reconnaissance. Other confusing designations are 10U (unmodified), 10S (standard), 10DC (drone carried—two converted to carry Ryan Firebees and allocated to Cold Lake experimental base), 10O (FM209 for Avro Orenda jet engine test-bed, burnt out and struck off charge July 24 1956) and 10C (Chinook test-bed FM205)—not flown.

Eleven Lancasters became instructional airframes with serials such as A515, 551B and 542C, whilst the only Avro (British) built Lancaster, a Mk III, EE182, was taken on charge on January 10 1944 and scrapped on March 4 1948. The only external variation in the basic marks, other than the varying array of radomes, camera ports and aerials, is the Mk 10AR which has a 36-inch nose extension to house the AN/APS-42B search radar, navigator and two of the ten fixed cameras. Like most modified Lancasters, the cockpit roof panel was solid, with some controls fitted. With their Arctic red warning panels they were perhaps the most colourful of all Lancasters and also served with No 408 Squadron at Rockcliffe along with No 413 Squadron as part of No 22 (Photographic) Wing of Air Transport Command until March 1964.

Maritime patrol squadrons were No 407 (based at Comox, British Columbia from July 1952 to May 1959), No 404 'Buffalo', coded 'AF', later 'SP', (April 1951—September 1955) and No 405 'Eagle', coded 'AG' (April 1950—November 1955), both the last based at Greenwood, Nova Scotia until their replacement by the Lockheed Neptune. As one of their duties, four Lancasters kept track of Arctic ice to safeguard shipping from early spring to late autumn. They were fairly frequent visitors to the United Kingdom.

Four squadrons of Lancaster bombers, Nos 37, 40, 70 and 104, were based in Egypt (Shallufa and Abu Sueir) from 1945 to 1947, patrolling the Canal Zone and carrying mail to England in bomb-bay panniers. The Lancasters left Bomber Command in 1950 when 49

The RCAF Lancaster 10MR, FM104, taxying in for a visit to RAF Scampton.

A close-up of the Dambusting mine mock-up fitted for the film.

Squadron lost its last example in March, becoming fully equipped with Lincolns.

Nos 82 and 541 Squadrons, with PR Mk 1 Lancasters, were formed for aerial survey in Africa, the last aircraft (PA427) being withdrawn in December 1953.

Coastal Command became the last RAF user as already related, St Mawgan, with No I School of Maritime Reconnaissance, training Shackleton crews until RF325, the last Lancaster in service was withdrawn on October 15 1956, and flown to Wroughton for scrapping. The Ministry of Supply kept NX739, a Mk VII, until January 1957 as a photographic mount, whilst PA474 was used at Cranfield College of Aeronautics for various tests, including that of the Handley-Page 'breathing' wing, an experiment to control the boundary layer. This latter aircraft is still kept airworthy by the Battle of Britain Memorial Flight now based at RAF Coningsby, Lincolnshire, a once-famous Lancaster base!

Many war surplus Lancasters were sold abroad, 15 B Mk 1s were brought out of storage for the Argentine Air Force in 1948 and coded B-031 to B-045, and nine more were sold to the Royal Egyptian Air Force, bearing

Mk 10AR with 33 in nose extension. White top, red cheat line with black edge and centre, white stripe. Otherwise natural metal (black as shown).

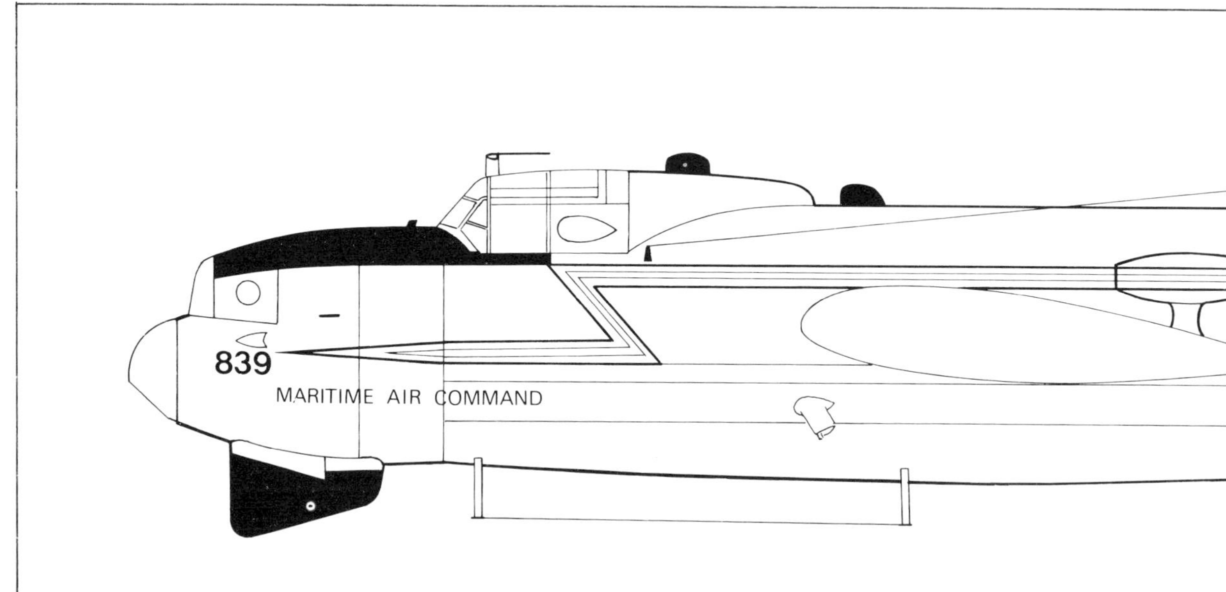

WU-01 was the first French Navy Lancaster, ex-613.

Arabic codes 1801/9, but it is not thought either Air Force made much use of them due to shortage of spares, bombs and ammunition.

Fifty-four Lancasters were supplied to L'Aeronavale under NATO defence plans in 1952. They comprised 32 Mk 1 and 22 Mk VII airframes all of which were brought up to RAF Maritime Reconnaissance standard at Langar, Nottinghamshire and Woodford, Cheshire. Bearing codes WU (Western Union) 01 to 54, they flew from bases in southern France and North Africa until 1961 and in the South Pacific (Noumea) until their retirement in 1964, one of the last, NX611, flying back to the United Kingdom in May 1965 to end its career as gate guardian at Scampton, Lincolnshire, first wartime base of the Dam Busters and where they still fly their Vulcans.

Five more Lancaster VIIs, with Lincoln undercarriages and rudders, were bought for air-sea rescue in the Mediterranean and based at Maison Blanche, Algeria and at Agadir in Morocco from December 1953.

The Lancaster was a most versatile aircraft, having a very strong airframe, and the last recorded use anywhere is when, at least two Mk Xs were converted as water bombers for fire control in Canadian forest areas, but details of their use are not available.

Many Lancasters were converted for use as jet engine test-beds as related earlier, and they also became film stars! The first movie appearance was in *Appointment in London*, in which the flying sequences were filmed at RAF Upwood. NX636, with blanked out nose, appeared in the film of Neville Shute's classic *No Highway* and PA474, wearing French markings, was also featured probably in a television series.

The major film must however be *The Dam Busters*, filmed at Hemswell. Four Mk VIIs were modified by having their bomb doors cut away and, as the actual weapon was still secret, a large sphere was hung in the gap, this being much oversize to emphasise its fitment during flying sequences. Other than the fact that the rear turret housed twin .5-inch Brownings instead of four .303-inch calibre, the results on film were as good as normally expected by movie-goers!

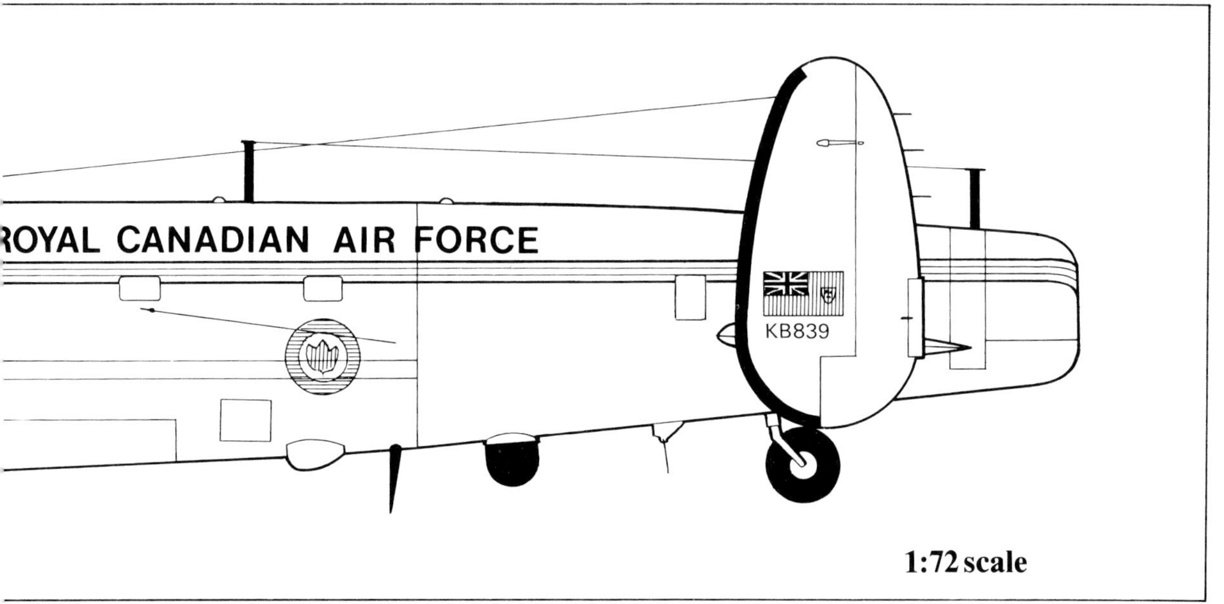

Chapter Seven

The Lanc at peace

It is difficult to determine who thought of using the Lancaster for civilian purposes, or when, but it is known that a Lancaster III, R5727, was flown to Malton in Canada in the August of 1942. There, Victory Aircraft faired over the nose and tail turrets and removed the mid-upper, fitted three new windows at the back, stripped off the camouflage paint and it became Fleet No 100 with Trans-Canada Air Lines. Experimental freight runs from Moncton to Goose Bay carrying loads up to 14,000 lb, proved the feasibility of the modifications. The aircraft was flown back to England and A.V. Roe & Co Ltd replaced the turrets with streamlined wooden fairings designed and supplied by Victory Aircraft. The nose cone was quite short and housed the navigator under a glazed top. Extra fuel tanks fitted in the bomb-bay increased the range to 4,000 miles and seats were fitted for ten passengers. Re-camouflaged and registered CF-CMS, 'Old TCA 100' inaugurated the TCA-operated Canadian Government Trans-Atlantic Air Service on July 22 1943, carrying four tons of mail from Dorval to Prestwick, non-stop, in just under $12\frac{1}{2}$ hours. A British Certificate of Airworthiness was granted for passenger carrying on September 1. Following this, two Canadian built Lancaster Xs were converted by TCA at Montreal, KB702 and KB703 becoming CF-CMT and CF-CMU, redesignated XPPs.

The Lancaster airmail drawing, reproduced, is dated December 1943 and it would seem that the Manchester drawing office, with the heat of preparing the Lancaster for production eased, had been able to prepare the new design. The forward mail compartment had a capacity of 2,000 lb, although the method by which mail bags could be packed in through the small hinged nose-cone, as shown, must have been draughtsman's licence! Seats for 12 passengers are shown although this arrangement did not come into use until the Lancastrian Mk 3. Standard seating was for nine passengers on three settees with their backs to the port fuselage wall—hence only windows on the starboard side. Three beds folded down from the roof, so only six passengers could sleep comfortably!

Six more Lancasters were converted for TCA by Victory Aircraft later in 1944, with the longer all-metal, semi-monocoque nose as shown on Avro's design drawing and these were referred to as 'Victorians'. These six were built as KB729/30 and FM184/7, becoming CF-CMV/NA, the first and the last three being transferred to Flight Refuelling Ltd through the Ministry of Civil Aviation, for use on the Berlin air lift in 1948 as G-AKDO/P/R/S, respectively, and designated Lancastrian Mk I.

The original conversion was burned out in a take-off accident at Dorval in June 1945 following its adaptation to take Merlin 85 engines (by Rolls-Royce at Hucknall). These Merlins were in circular, Lancaster VI-type cowlings as later used in the DC-4M Argonaut, the airliner which replaced the Lancastrian on the Atlantic route in 1947. One of the earlier conversions was lost on the Atlantic in December 1944 with British Admiralty

FM187 became Lancastrian CF-CNA and, later, G-AKDS with Flight Refuelling. Note the absence of carburettor air intakes on the cowling side with Merlin T24/4 engines in TMD power plants. The canopy has been modified (Roy Cross).

officials, but the remaining six kept up a twice-weekly schedule across the Atlantic. Up to September 16 1946 the service was from Dorval to Prestwick but it was then extended to London as a public service, although uneconomic. Nearly 2,000 flights were made before being replaced by unpressurised but sound-proofed Canadair C-4s, basically Merlin-engined Douglas DC-4s. It is interesting to note that later pressurised versions of this aircraft, the Argonaut, were purchased for Atlantic service on the failure of the Avro Tudor!

Following the success of these Canadian conversions, a slightly developed version with 500-gallon fuel tanks in the forward bomb-bay was put into production at Manchester in 1944 as the Avro 691 (the Tudor was the Avro 689 and first flew on June 14 1945). It was intended for use on the Australian route until the Tudors came along and the first Lancastrian I, as it was designated, G-AGLF ex-VB873, was delivered to Hurn for the BOAC Development Flight and received its C of A on February 7 1945. In April, this machine made a record-breaking flight to New Zealand in three and a half days! Pre-war services had taken up to four times as long, today it takes 30 hours and Concorde will halve this!

On January 20 1944 the first British-built Lancaster to be civilianised, DV379, camouflaged and with neat fairings in place of nose and tail turrets, was handed over to BOACs newly-created Development Flight at Hurn. It had been allocated for conversion in November of the previous year, becoming G-AGJI, and was employed to test a variety of new equipment for post-war airliners under development. Its original Merlin 22 engines were exchanged for T24s by Rolls-Royce at Hucknall as these were the power units used in Lancastrians. From its Croydon base, G-AGJI returned to Hucknall in May 1945 to receive Merlin 102 engines with annular radiators in Tudor-type cowlings. The camouflage was removed at Hurn the same year at its first post-war C of A overhaul and it received the usual BOAC colours. It gave good service until November 1946 and was broken up at Colerne late the following year.

Twenty Lancastrians from the end of Lancaster production were delivered to BOAC by October 1945 although 32 had been ordered. These were registered from G-AGLS to 'GMM ('I' was not used) and operated jointly with QUANTAS on the Kangaroo service, in Transport Command markings, with Australian crews taking over at Karachi. The first scheduled service left Hurn on the last day of May 1945 flown by G-AGLV coded 'OKZV' and serialled VF163, while the westbound machine G-AGLS, 'OKZS', VD238, left Sydney on June 2. Despite an estimated annual loss of £1,400,000 the Kangaroo service was deemed worthwhile for prestige purposes, although each aircraft carried only nine passengers and a limited amount of mail.

Before World War 2, France, Germany and Italy had all served South America by air but, until the advent of

BOAC's G-AGMD, in sprightly mood, shows its wing registration letters.

the Lancastrian, Britain did not have a commercial aircraft with sufficient range for the South Atlantic crossing. Hence, when senior BOAC Captain O.P. Jones left Hurn in G-AGMG 'Nicosia' to survey the route to Buenos Aires and over the Andes to Santiago and Lima, an ambition was realised. With the formation of British South American Airways Corporation, using six Lancastrian 3s, G-AGWG/L, carrying up to 13 passengers each, a regular service was opened in 1946.

BOAC civil Lancaster 1, ex-DV379, at Hucknall, with Merlin T24s installed and awaiting conversion to Merlin 102s. The engineless Lancaster in the background is EE134, coded CE-O (Rolls-Royce Ltd).

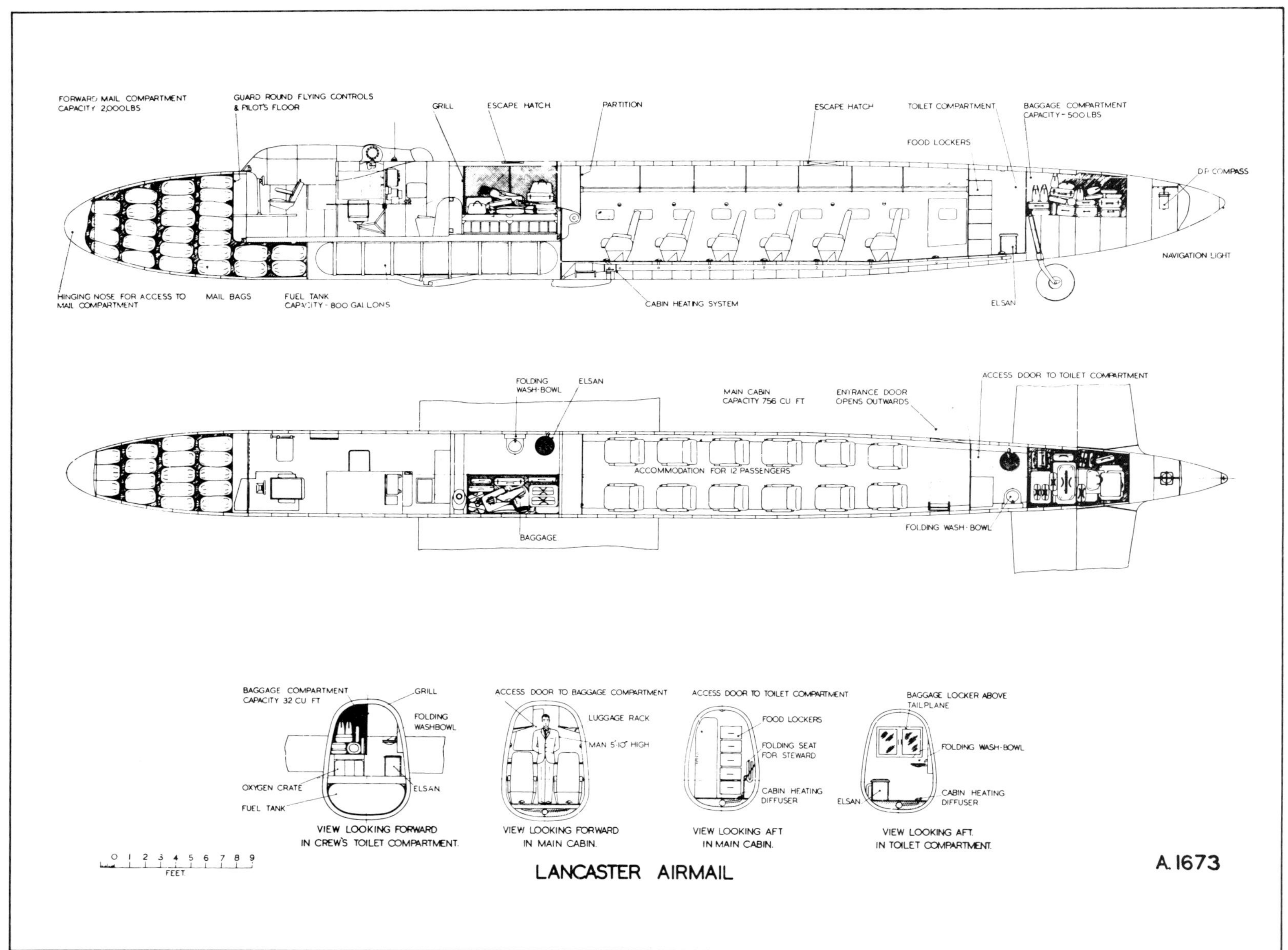

FORWARD MAIL COMPARTMENT CAPACITY 2,000 LBS
GUARD ROUND FLYING CONTROLS & PILOT'S FLOOR
GRILL
ESCAPE HATCH
PARTITION
ESCAPE HATCH
TOILET COMPARTMENT
FOOD LOCKERS
BAGGAGE COMPARTMENT CAPACITY - 500 LBS
DF. COMPASS
NAVIGATION LIGHT
HINGING NOSE FOR ACCESS TO MAIL COMPARTMENT
MAIL BAGS
FUEL TANK CAPACITY - 800 GALLONS
CABIN HEATING SYSTEM
ELSAN
FOLDING WASH-BOWL
ELSAN
MAIN CABIN CAPACITY 756 CU FT
ENTRANCE DOOR OPENS OUTWARDS
ACCESS DOOR TO TOILET COMPARTMENT
ACCOMMODATION FOR 12 PASSENGERS
FOLDING WASH-BOWL
BAGGAGE
BAGGAGE COMPARTMENT CAPACITY 32 CU FT
GRILL
FOLDING WASHBOWL
OXYGEN CRATE
FUEL TANK
ELSAN
VIEW LOOKING FORWARD IN CREW'S TOILET COMPARTMENT.
ACCESS DOOR TO BAGGAGE COMPARTMENT
LUGGAGE RACK
MAN 5'10" HIGH
VIEW LOOKING FORWARD IN MAIN CABIN.
ACCESS DOOR TO TOILET COMPARTMENT
FOOD LOCKERS
FOLDING SEAT FOR STEWARD
CABIN HEATING DIFFUSER
VIEW LOOKING AFT IN MAIN CABIN.
BAGGAGE LOCKER ABOVE TAILPLANE
FOLDING WASH-BOWL
ELSAN
CABIN HEATING DIFFUSER
VIEW LOOKING AFT. IN TOILET COMPARTMENT.
0 1 2 3 4 5 6 7 8 9 FEET
LANCASTER AIRMAIL
A.1673

Meanwhile, the Royal Air Force, with overseas commitments in India, Australia and the Far East, had ordered 33 Lancastrian C 2s as an interim long-range transport to Air Ministry specification C 16/44. (Of 23 Lancaster C Is ordered earlier, 21 had been transferred to BOAC, in 1945 and two, VH737 and VH742, had become Nene test-beds with Rolls-Royce). These Lancastrians, fitted with Merlin T 24 engines, still had only nine seats, and were built at Woodford being delivered between October 1945 and March 1946. They entered service at Full Sutton with the Lancastrian Training Unit. Civilian pilots also received familiarisation with this unit which eventually became No 231 Squadron. The Handling Squadron of the Empire Central Flying School received two aircraft, VM728 and VM729 and another, VL968 joined the Empire Air Navigation School at Shawbury which was already using Lancaster PD328, 'Aries I', fitted with Lancastrian-type nose and tail cone. No 232 Squadron based at Palan in India received VM733/5; VM701 joined the Yorks of No 511 Squadron at Lyneham and most of the remainder served with No 1359 (VIP) Flight at Lyneham and later at Bassingbourn. By the end of 1948 most had been converted and sold for civil use to BOAC, BSAAC, Skyways, and Flight Refuelling Ltd, those that remained being with No 24 Squadron which had absorbed No 1359 Flight in June 1946. At least seven were used experimentally for engine test-beds as related elsewhere.

'Aries I' began its flying career in 1944 by circumnavigating the Earth in 40 days, covering a total distance of over 47,000 miles during the journey and, incidentally, also establishing a new record to the Cape. In all, 'Aries I' flew nearly 200,000 miles, or the equivalent of seven more flights round the world. It made liaison trips to Canada and the United States in 1945 and, two days after VE day, left on one of the most spectacular flights ever made at the time—over the North geographic and magnetic poles. When it returned after two weeks, it had flown a total of 28,700 miles, of which nearly 20,000 had been over Arctic regions. In 1946, the last year of its career, 'Aries I' established official records on the route from London to Karachi, London to Darwin, and London to Wellington. It also flew non-stop from Cairo to the Cape. In the autumn of that year, before being disposed of in January 1947, a

liaison flight was made to Canada and the USA.

Eight Lancastrian C Mk 4s, TX283/90, were built at Yeadon and delivered from March 8 to April 2 1946, these being equivalent to civilian 10/13-seat 3s. Three of these, TX287/9, were overhauled for Flota Aerea Mercante Argentina (FAMA) as LV-ACU, S and V; all transferred to the air force in 1949 as VIP transports with the V Brigada Aeria at Villa Mercedes.

A total of 80 Lancastrians was produced, the last 18, ordered as Lancastrian 3s by BSAAC, although only six, G-AGNG/L were delivered due to the airline being

Above *The prototype Lancaster C1, VB673, later G-AGLF with BOAC.*

Top *Silver City's 'City of London', G-AHBW, arriving in Malta after its record-breaking flight from London on December 16 1946. It took 4 hours 10 minutes.*

Below *'Aries', PD328, being refuelled and serviced under armed guard at Blackbushe in 1946.*

absorbed by BOAC. Of the remaining 12, five, G-AHBX/Y, 'HCB, 'HCD and 'HCE, were collected by the newly formed British European Airways Corporation for Alitalia Aerolinee Italiane Internazionale, a partly British-owned company. They became I-AHBX, I-AHBY, I-AHCB, I-AHCD and I-DALR respectively and were used for a weekly Rome—Buenos Aires service which commenced on June 2 1948, with stops at Dakar, Natal, Rio de Janeiro and Montevideo. Total flying time was 30 hours with, altogether, five and a half hours on the ground at the four stops mentioned. A Lancaster B 1/Spec had been purchased earlier as crew trainer and this aircraft, PP741, unusual in that its 22,000 lb bomb-bay was enclosed by double curvature doors and still fitted with turrets, was flown into White Waltham in July 1947 and received G-AJWM and 'ALITALIA-ROMA' in white before being ferried out on November 30 1948.

The other seven, three of which—G-AHBT, HBV and HBW—formed the initial equipment of Silver City Airways and G-AHBU, Z, 'HCA and C sold to Skyways, were used for charter flights to South Africa, Australia and the Far East. Skyways also bought eight ex-RAF Lancastrian C 2/4s during 1947 and 1948 and five were sold to BOAC for use on their South American service after the failure of the Tudor.

Six Lancasters had been acquired by BSAAC in 1946 for freight use and four of these, PP688/90 and PP751, were converted at Bracebridge Heath with Lancastrian type noses, bulged bomb doors and stripped out fuselages to increase their carrying capacity, although the rear turrets were just sprayed over. They were registered G-AGUJ/M and named 'Star Pilot', 'Star Gold', 'Star Watch' and 'Star Ward' respectively. They

flew for a year, carrying perishable goods and South American cotton crop samples but, due to their limited capacity, proved uneconomical. G-AGUL crashed at Heathrow on October 23 1947, 'UK was reduced to spares at Langley the same year, 'UJ followed two years later but the last, 'UM was reprieved and used by Airtech Ltd at Thame for the development of an outsize pannier to carry vehicles and outsize loads during the Berlin airlift and was dismantled at Dunsfold in 1949. The two unconverted Lancasters, PP744 and PP746, allocated G-AGUN and G-AGUO, were returned to the RAF, the first eventually being civilianised in July 1946 as G-AHVN to replace G-AGJI with the BOAC Development Flight.

QANTAS took over three of BOACs original Lancastrians, G-AGMD (VF155) 'Nairn', 'GML (VF147) 'Nicobar', 'GLZ (VF167) 'Nottingham' and Silver City's G-AHBW 'City of London' as VH-EAS/V and, from December 16 1947, started a weekly flight for the RAAF from Sydney to Japan. A ventral pannier to carry spare Merlin power plants was fitted to one of these Lancastrians and the service extended to Tokyo in October 1948. The first direct flight to South Africa was made in November via the Cocos Islands and Mauritius.

The Berlin airlift extended the Lancastrian's life until 1951 with Flight Refuelling Ltd adapting 14 aircraft for the bulk delivery of petrol and oil with 2,500-gallon fuselage tanks. A total of 5,600 sorties was made by the combined fleet, five from BOAC, four from TCA as mentioned earlier, and five from Skyways. Four Skyways Lancastrians had, during the 1947 milk shortage, carried churns from Belfast to Liverpool and perhaps this was the most unusual load for the erstwhile heavy bomber! After the airlift, the Lancastrians were

The colour scheme of a civil airline Lanc. Wide dark blue line topped by three light blue lines. ALITALIA written in light blue. The bow and arrow are dark blue and light blue. The name and registration letters are black. Overall natural metal.

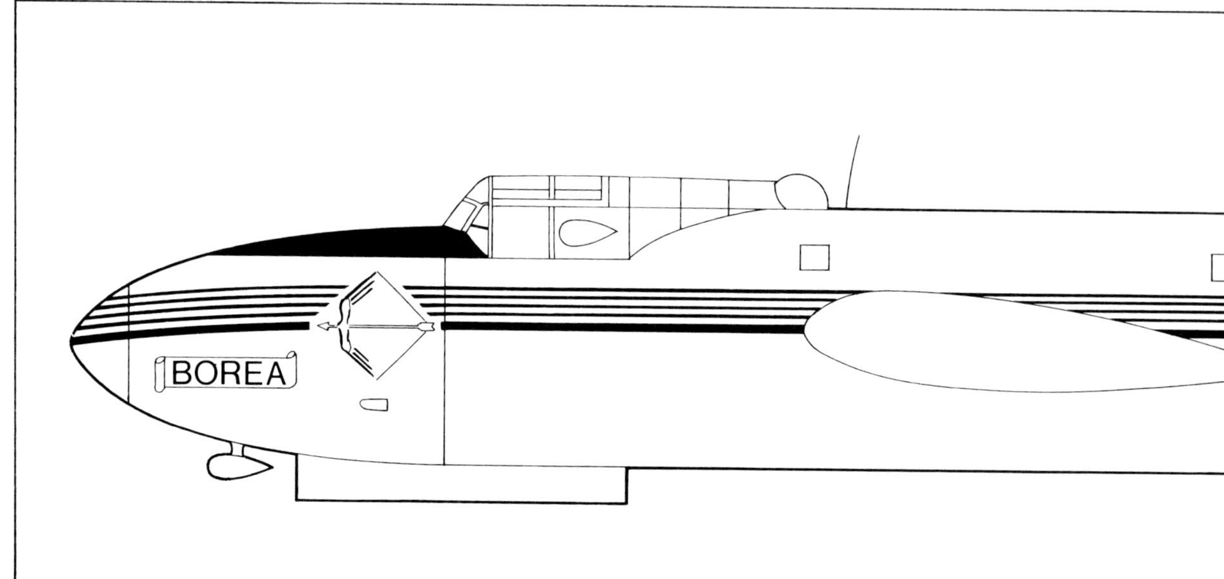

Flight Refuelling's Lancaster BIII conversion, G-AHJU, at an RAeS garden party in Radlett, September 15 1946 (The Beaumont Collection).

flown back to their bases at Hurn, Dunsfold and Tarrant Rushton and were scrapped in 1951.

Also an attempt was made in 1948 by Onzeair Ltd to establish a charter company using four Lancastrians, CF-CMW and X from TCA and two Skyways aircraft, G-AJPP and G-AJKO. Medical supplies were ferried from London but, due to some suspicion of gun-running and the loss of 'MW near the end of its delivery flight from Montreal via London on August 1, the operation was wound up.

Flight Refuelling Ltd made extensive use of four Lancaster B IIIs, LL809, 681, 639 and ED866, which they acquired from the RAF in August 1946. They were converted into tanker and receiver aircraft at Staverton, with bulk storage tanks and power driven hose reels, and operated from Ford to perfect the company's airborne refuelling techniques following the earlier use of Lancaster IIIs, NE147, ND648 and PB972. Originally

used in bomber colours, with large yellow civil registrations, G-AHJT/W respectively, they later lost their wartime camouflage and flew unpainted. 22 flight refuelled trips were made across the Atlantic from May 28 to August 1947. The first, flown by Flight Refuelling's managing director, Air Vice-Marshal D.C.T. Bennett, of Pathfinder fame, left Heathrow, received 1,700 gallons of fuel from an Azores-based Lancaster tanker in mid-Atlantic and landed in Bermuda after a 3,355 mile non-stop flight. As is well known, the Royal Air Force eventually adopted the Flight Refuelling probe and drogue system for their V-force and fighters, perhaps the most notable flights being those by Harriers in the Trans-Atlantic Air Race in May 1969. Despite successful trials by American B-29s, the USAF adopted their own boom system.

Modifications to produce the Lancastrian were quite simple and mainly involved the extension of the fuselage

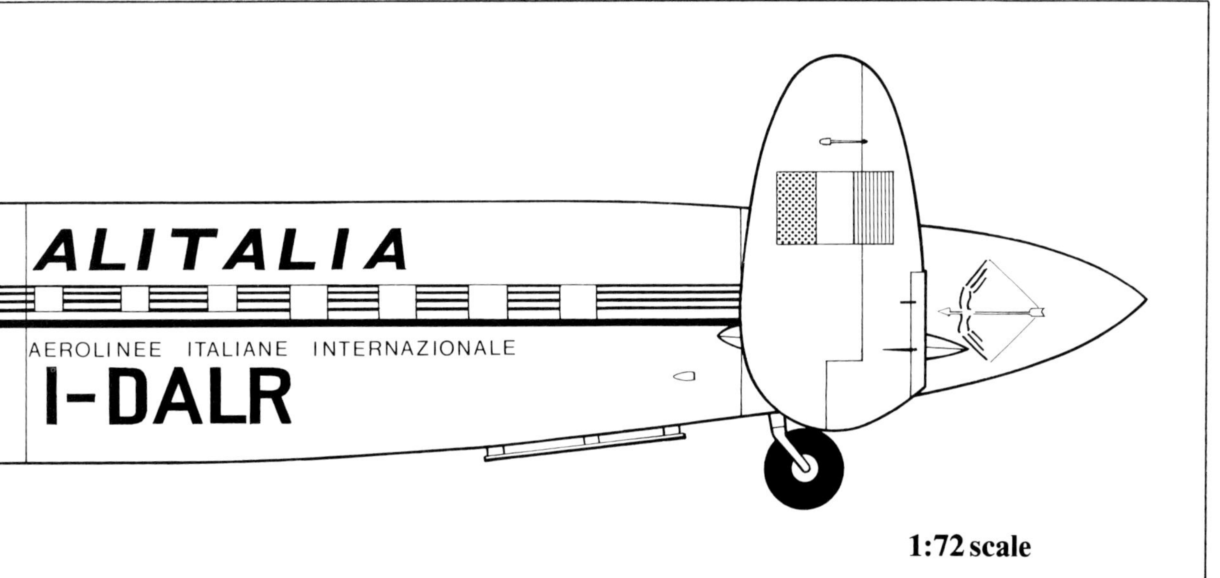

to 76 feet 10 inches. The original bomber nose was replaced, forward of former 'E', where the section was 6 feet high and 5 feet wide, by a new stream-lined nose approximately 12 feet long, terminating in an upward-hinged cargo door secured at the bottom by two bolts. This new section could carry up to 2,275 lb and had four lashing points to secure the load. The pilot's cabin was dimensionally identical with the Lancaster, 13 feet long, 6 feet high at the front under the canopy and 4 feet 6 inches at the rear. First and Second Pilots were accommodated, the latter having a collapsible seat so that access could be made forward. The Flight Engineer's seat was behind the First Pilot, facing his panel on the starboard cockpit wall. The Navigator was provided with a table similar to the Lancaster, but slightly shorter, again on the left-hand side of the fuselage, his seat being on the right, and the Wireless Operator sat immediately in front of the main spar facing forward.

Between the wing spars, the forward toilet compartment was about 7 feet long and 5 feet 6 inches wide, whilst the galley, of similar size, was behind the rear spar and included a refrigerator, electric hot-water urn, drinking water filter, steward's seat, etc. Access to the passenger cabin was through a door on the starboard side in a bulkhead at former 17. The passenger compartment, panelled, like the galley in plywood and sound-proofed with glass wool, was 20 feet long, 4 feet 6 inches wide and 6 feet 3 inches high above the floor on the centre-line. In earlier versions, nine passengers sat facing to the right and to the windows. Later versions, with windows on both sides, but no galley, had up to 14 seats arranged in a conventional manner, but only for short-range comfort! A small cloakroom, 6 feet by 2 feet by 20 inches, which also housed an H or J type dinghy in a BOAC valise, was immediately opposite the entrance door, with the rear toilet compartment, 6 feet high, 3 feet 6 inches wide and 3 feet 6 inches long, between the cloakroom and tail-plane. At the rear, the luggage compartment was 6 feet 6 inches long, 3 feet high and 3 feet 6 inches wide, with a maximum stowage of 410 lb, and the D R compass was fitted right in the pointed tail-cone, with access through a door in the rear bulkhead when in flight.

A forward mail compartment, 5 feet 6 inches long and 2 feet 6 inches high at its highest point, could carry up to 630 lb and was below the pilot's cabin floor with access through a door on the port side of the nose. No bomb-bay was fitted, the front section housed two fuel tanks each of 504 gallons capacity, while the rear floor usually found in the Lancaster was cut back for the passenger cabin.

Brief mention should be made of two long-distance flights made by Lancastrian C 2s of the Empire Air Navigation School at Shawbury where they were used as long-range navigation trainers. Leaving Blackbushe on November 12 1945, Air Vice-Marshal Fiddament in VM701 covered 34,000 miles on a round the world flight in 36 days. Squadron Leader J. Adam flew VM726 from Northolt to Wellington, New Zealand, a journey of 12,500 miles, in March 1946 and returned to Northolt $157\frac{1}{4}$ hours after leaving, the first circumnavigation of the world in less than seven days.

Despite its earlier design, Avro 685, the York mainly replaced the Lancastrian—so to the last of the Manchester line.

Mail going aboard 'Star Trail', G-AGWK of BSAA, at Heathrow circa 1947.

Chapter Eight

The York

With Avro type number 685, the York was conceived by designer Roy Chadwick to exploit more fully the long distance load carrying capability of the Lancaster. Using the same wing, tail unit, undercarriage and power units, but with a completely new square section fuselage having twice the volume of the original, the first prototype, LV626, took to the air at Ringway on July 5 1942, only five months after drawings were supplied to Avro's experimental department. It had been produced almost unofficially as, due to the US agreement, neither material or labour was available for the manufacture of transport aircraft. However, the camouflaged prototype, still with only the Lancaster's twin fins, was successfully tested at Boscombe Down and three further development prototypes and a small production batch were ordered as York C Mk Is to Air Ministry Specification 1/42.

During World War 2, an agreement was reached with the American Government that all transport aircraft for the Royal Air Force would be supplied as Lend-Lease equipment, thus leaving British industry to concentrate on military aircraft. This worked very well, and reverse Lend-Lease gave the Americans Beaufighters, Spitfires, Mosquitos, Horsa gliders, etc, whilst the ubiquitous Dakota was handed over in thousands. Obviously, the British aviation industry, even when reorganised and put on a war footing by Lord Beaverbrook, could not have coped with transport aircraft in addition to the fleets of four-engined bombers, but it did leave a large gap in our post-war requirements! It has been said, perhaps unkindly and untruthfully, that the Yanks knew what they were doing. Skymasters and Connies were developed and built in quantity, even the flying boat was nearly forgotten and we finished the war without any hopes of getting transport aircraft delivered quickly.

The Brabazon Committee had been set up in 1943 with this need in mind, but early results were not up to expectations, the Dove being perhaps the only really successful aircraft to come forward. The mammoth Brabazon itself, and the Princess flying boat both took too long to develop, the Ambassador and Marathon were not adopted in quantity. This left the Viking development of the Wellington to soldier on until we got back on our feet with the successful Viscount, and later, Comet, when its earlier troubles were rectified.

The third prototype York, the first to be fitted with the familiar central fin, had square instead of round windows, and was delivered to No 24 Squadron at

The spacious cockpit layout of the York prototype in July 1942.

Top *Tail detail showing access door.*

Above *LV633 'Ascalon' runs up at Langar.*

Below *An uncoded York showing the freight doors. Dark green/brown, sky blue.*

Hendon in March 1953 as LV633 'Ascalon' (St George's sword) and camouflaged dark green/earth with black undersides, for the use of Winston Churchill. This prototype had been designed in November 1942 as an Air Yacht but this was later changed to a York (Special), furnished as a flying conference room. A pressure cabin, to an RAE design, was built by A. V. Roe but was never installed. On May 25 1943 'Ascalon' took the Prime Minister and Allied commanders to Algiers, via Gibraltar and, a few days later, flew H M King George VI to visit his troops in North Africa and the Mediterranean.

With output stepped up to three per month in 1944, the first production Yorks, MW100/1 joined No 24 Squadron in May but it was not until the next year that No 511 Squadron at Lyneham became the first to be completely equipped, full quantity production having started. This was to continue until April 1958 when the 258th and last York, PE108, was delivered from Woodford. MW100 replaced 'Ascalon' when the latter was transferred to the Far East Communications Flight at Singapore in 1946 and served until 1953 when it was replaced by 'Ascalon II', another VIP York, MW295, the last to be retired from the RAF in March 1957 when it was flown home and put up for sale.

Early production VIP Yorks included MW102 for Lord Louis Mountbatten, Commander-in-Chief South-East Asia, MW107, later '4999', named 'Oubaas' with the South African Air Force for Field Marshal Jan Smuts and MW140 used in Australia by the Duke of Gloucester when he was Governor-General in 1945-46 and named 'Endeavour'. Other VIP Yorks were used by Field Marshal Montgomery and General de Gaulle, whilst it is interesting to note that the first two

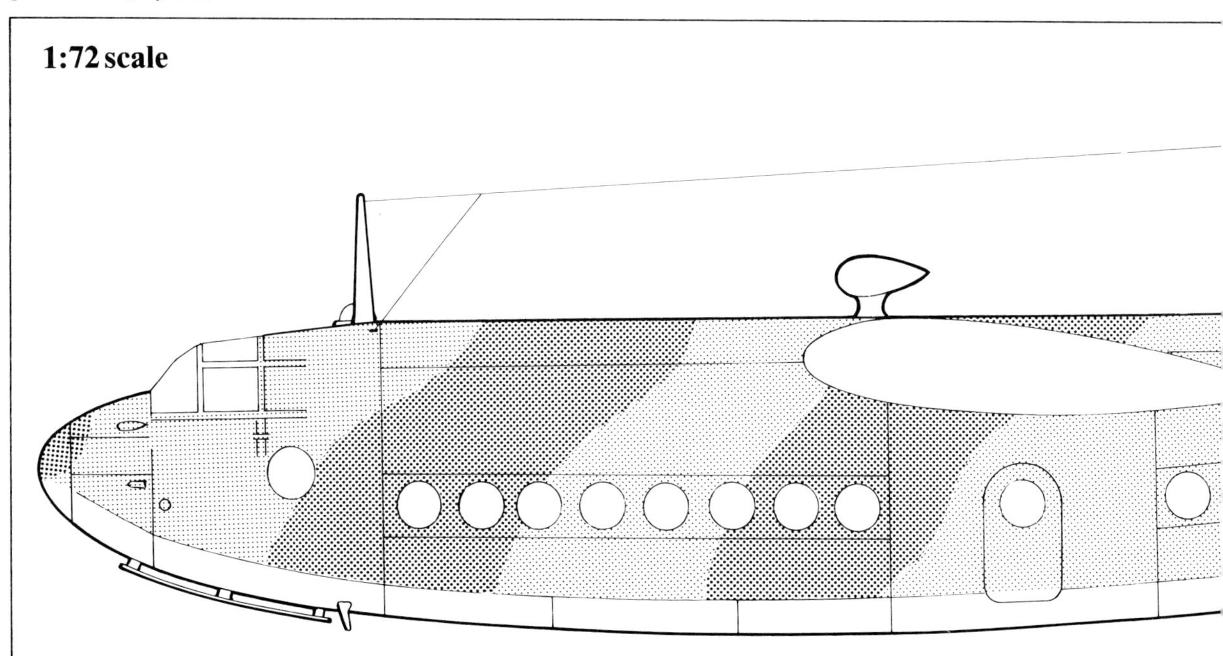

A side view of an uncoded York showing freight doors.

production VIP Yorks (MW100/1) covered over half a million miles between them, carrying many important people to conferences all over the world—Teheran, Cairo, Moscow and Yalta being among places that spring to mind.

In addition to the four prototypes, 208 Yorks were supplied to the Royal Air Force, an initial order for 200 and eight only from a further 100 ordered. Ten squadrons were equipped, Nos 40, 51, 59, 99, 206, 232, 242 and 246 in addition to those already mentioned, whilst 241 OCU, 1332(T) and 1384(T) conversion units used the York, as did the Indian HQ Communications Flight. Strangely enough, the York was not designed as a military type and its achievements during the Berlin airlift 30 years ago are perhaps a story of their own.

During Operation Plainfare, the York was the first aircraft on the airlift and 40 were used from June 24 1948 to September 30 1949, all seven of the then current York squadrons being involved. Some 29,000 flights were made to Berlin and over 230,000 tons of supplies were carried, that is nearly half of the total RAF contribution of half a million tons. The RAF made almost 66,000 flights and other aircraft used included 50 Dakotas, 14 Hastings, and two squadrons of Sunderlands. What a pity that the airlift memorial at Templehof does not display a York as well as a Douglas C-54 and Hastings—at least the American sign does acknowledge the York along with the Skymaster!

Five early passenger/freighter versions of the York were diverted from RAF production in 1944, these being MW103, MW108, MW113, MW121 and MW129 which became G-AGJA/E. The first, still camouflaged, received its Certificate of Airworthiness on February 21. With a rear cabin housing 12 passengers and a forward freight hold, they were initially used on a UK/Middle East service from April 22. Production at Ringway

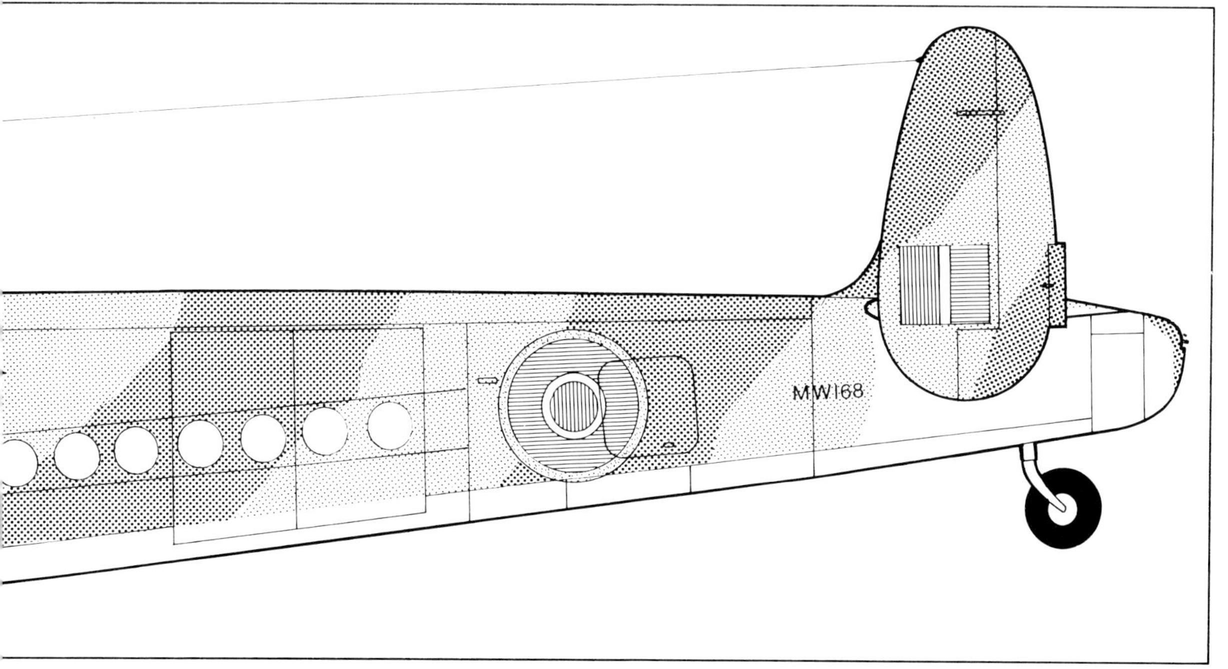

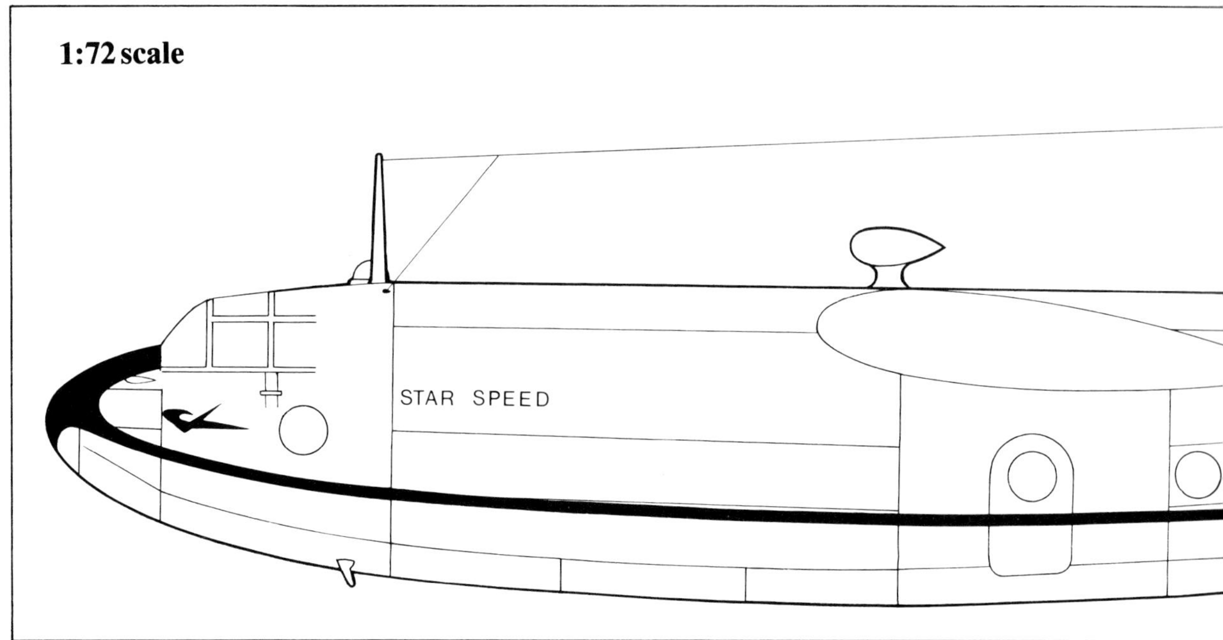

This York, in service with BSAA, had blue trim and black letters. Overall natural metal.

ceased in October 1945 when the jigs were transferred to Avro's Yeadon shadow factory where the last 77 Yorks were built. The last 45 were all to civilian orders although 25 were operated jointly by BOAC and the RAF, allocated TS789 to TS813. Twelve went to British South American Airways as G-AHEW/FH, five went to FAMA, already operating the uneconomic 12-seat Lancastrian, and were fitted out as 24-seaters, whilst three 30-passenger aircraft were bought by Skyways Ltd. These were registered G-AHFI, 'HLV and 'JUP named 'Skyway', 'Sky Courier' and 'Sky Consul' respectively, the first being lost when it crashed at Gatow in March 1949 during the Berlin airlift, after flying 147 sorties. A fourth York, the only Canadian-built example, FM400, notable for having its windows parallel to the ground, was also bought by Skyways and used as G-ALBX 'Sky Dominion' and flew 467 sorties before crashing at Wunsdorf on June 19 1949.

The BOAC aircraft, originally wearing Transport Command four-letter codes, similar to the Lancastrians, eg, G-AGJA ex-MW103, carried 'OY-ZA', were released by the RAF in 1946 and received civil livery of BOAC blue, gold and polished metal and became the 'M' class (the Lancastrians had been the 'N' class—G-AGLZ was 'Nottingham'). Thirteen of these aircraft were fitted out as 12-berth sleepers for the 'Springbok' service to Johannesburg, five being used by South African Airways in 1946-47.

Most of the RAF Yorks used in Operation Plainfare were retired and broken up at Aldergrove, Kirkbride and Silloth but many airlines and charter operators bought up some 40 ex-RAF Yorks when they were replaced by the Hastings from 1952 onwards and they appeared in many

colours and under many flags. Early in 1948, the India-Pakistan airlift used Yorks for the evacuation of British and European families from Pakistan, possibly carrying a record passenger load when 117 fleeing emigrants were carried from Pakistan with, needless to say, all the seats removed! During this operation, the York was indirectly responsible for saving thousands of lives; 400 members of the Palestine Police Force were ferried to Malaya in Yorks, over 100 tons of grain were dropped to starving Arabs in Hadramout, Southern Arabia in February 1949 by York frieghters. Earlier, during the milk shortage in England in the hard winter of 1947-48, Yorks, helped by sister Lancastrians, as related elsewhere, made four round trips a day to Ireland, each with a load of 1,450 gallons ($6\frac{1}{4}$ tons). This helped to put milk on the table in many homes during this rough period and could only have been achieved by flying it in!

As a weight-lifter, the York inherited a lot from the Lancaster and this was well illustrated in April 1950 when Eagle Aviation aircraft carried the largest single cargo then transported by air. The Greek tanker *John Chandris* was stranded in a Dutch ship repair yard with a broken propeller shaft. A replacement 18 feet long and weighing 21,000 lb ($9\frac{1}{2}$ tons) was needed urgently. A York did the job! Military freighter Yorks could carry four Jeeps which were loaded up a simple ramp.

Another notable record for the York was created during Operation Longstop, an RAF exercise in September 1947 when 20 Yorks and four spare aircraft had a 100 per cent serviceability record, the only ones out of the 96 aircraft used in the exercise!

After having flown some 172,000 hours (nearly 20 years!) and covered over 13 million miles, BOAC retired

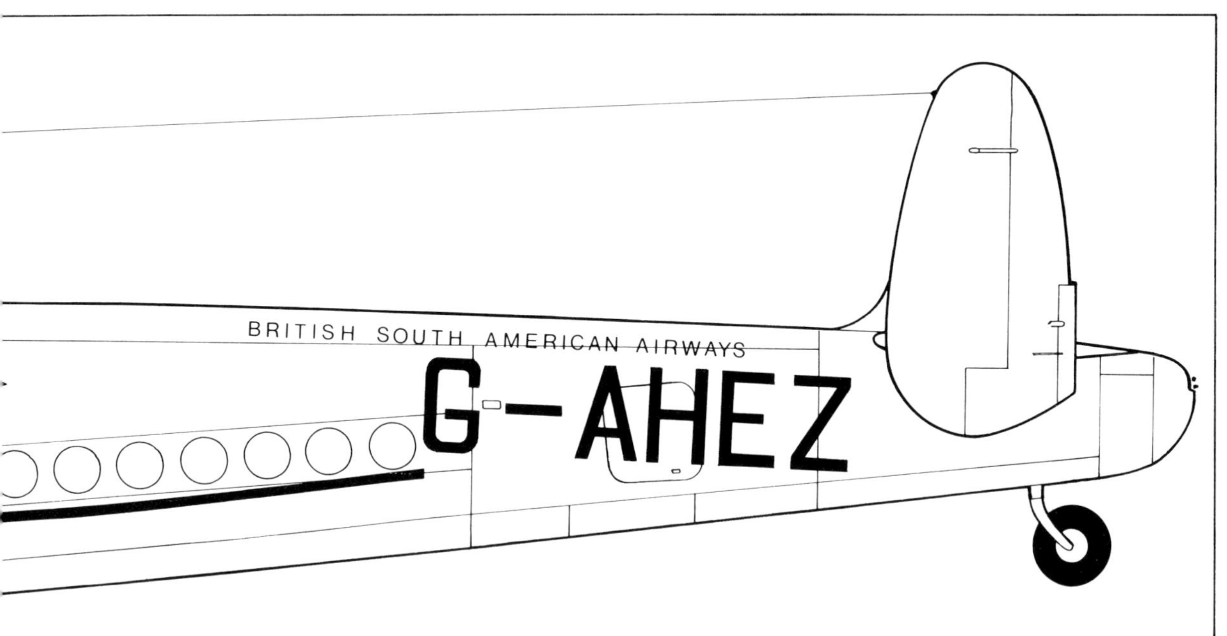

its Avro Yorks from passenger carrying operations from October 7 1950. Considering that the Yorks had originally only been put in service as a stop-gap aircraft pending the availability of the Avro Tudor, later replaced by the Canadair DC-4M long-range pressurised aircraft, this is not a bad record! The first British South American Airways York, 'Star Leader', flew a charter flight to Venezuela for Shell Petroleum before replacing Lancastrians on the South Atlantic route to Buenos Aires. On June 11 1946 G-AHEW returned to Heathrow via Bermuda and Gander covering the last leg of over 2,200 miles with a full load of 21 passengers and seven crew in 10 hours 35 minutes, the first commercial flight on this route. After leasing further Yorks from BOAC, competition and several tragic losses forced BSAA to cease operation and nine of the original 12 Yorks were taken over by BOAC on July 30 1949.

FAMA had introduced its five Yorks in a joint service with Iberia on September 22 1946, which continued until the South American airline was absorbed by Aerolineas Argentinas in May 1949. Their three surviving Yorks continued to operate until bought by Eagle Aviation in December 1950, to join three others from the BSAA/BOAC fleet which had been in service since October 1949. Two of the Argentine Yorks were sold to Surrey Flying Services and 21 of the BOAC fleet (a few were kept for training, freighting and carrying of spare engines) were purchased by the Lancashire Aircraft Corporation between May 1951 and August 1952. Some of these Yorks were used in the airlifting of troops to the Canal Zone at the end of 1951, using RAF serials in the WW range to meet the terms of the 1936 Anglo-Egyptian Treaty which banned civil aircraft.

Skyways Ltd which had not operated since the end of the Berlin airlift late in 1949, was bought by Lancashire Aircraft Corporation and their Yorks were operated under the title 'Skyways of London', the parent company concentrating on operating DC-3s and other smaller types from their Blackpool base. The British equestrian Olympic team was flown to the Games at Helsinki in 1952 and promptly won—obviously their horses did not object to the noisy York!

Four of the surplus RAF Yorks were bought by Air Charter Ltd, a company in Freddie Laker's Aviation Traders group, which also took over Surrey Flying Services, giving a fleet of eight Yorks with three others being used for spares. Air Charter used their fleet in 1953 for the evacuation of East German refugees from Berlin to West Germany before the Wall was closed and, later that year, obtained a 12-month War Office contract for a fortnightly London—Fiji trooping service.

Scottish Aviation also bought eight ex-RAF Yorks and fitted some of them with 50 rearward facing seats for trooping, using others for a regular trans-Atlantic charter freight service from Prestwick as Scottish Airlines.

Hunting also bought a fleet of Yorks, four from the RAF, two of which were used for spares, and some from other operators, to open up a UK—Africa freight service under the Hunting-Clan Air Transport banner in July 1955.

Dan-Air Ltd, actually the last York operator, formed in March 1953, bought three in July of the next year, the first being converted by Scottish Aviation. Receipt of an Air Ministry freight contract in 1956 for a London—Singapore service necessitated the conversion of the other two and purchase of others, whilst a regular nightly freight service operated for BEA served London—Manchester and Glasgow until Argosies were introduced in 1961. Their last York, G-ANTK, was presented to the local Air Scouts at Lesham in 1964 but is

The prototype LV626 re-equipped with Hercules engines.

now preserved by its former owner.

The last two BOAC Yorks, G-AGJC and G-AGSO, were retired in November 1967 after 13 years of service in which they had covered a total of 44 million miles, carrying 90,000 passengers and had flown nearly 227,000 hours. They were purchased by Skyways Ltd then operated from Stansted. This company remained the largest York operator, flying a service between London, Malta and Cyprus until 1957. Other Yorks were leased to Middle East operators, Aden and Arab Airways, and to Saudi Arabia where they were used for the expanding pilgrim traffic to Mecca. Three Yorks were sold to Persian Air Services Ltd and used for freighting between Beirut, Teheran and the oil centres of Abadan and Kuwait, as well as to Basle, Switzerland via Brindisi, whilst others were leased to Air Liban and Middle East Airlines, the latter having BOAC interests. A third Lebanese operator was TMA (Trans Mediterranean Airways) which had bought two ex-VIP Yorks, 'Oubaas', once Smuts' aircraft, this becoming OD-ACN with 54 folding seats, and 'Ascalon II', the last RAF aircraft which, after conversion by Field Aircraft Services, became OD-ACQ in June 1957.

Three Yorks were purchased from the Air Ministry by Aéronavale in 1954, these being MW137, MW243 and MW265, used as military freighters under codes PA 1/3 respectively, from Le Bourget.

In 1954, 12 Yorks were overhauled by the makers for use in northern Canada during the construction of the Distant Early Warning (DEW) Line along the Arctic Circle. Eleven were ex-RAF, the other was bought from Air Charter and Spartan Air Services of Ottawa, and they were allocated registrations CF-HAS, HFP/Q, HMU/Z and HTM on January 21 1955, by the DoT of Canada. These Yorks were prepared for their Atlantic flight at RAF Kilbride and then ferried from Silloth to Ottawa.

G-AGJB, ex-MW BOAC's 'Marathon' runs up its engines.

They were operated by Arctic Airways, later Trans Air, Associated Airways, Maritime Central Airways and Pacific Western Airlines, at least nine of them being written off in the rugged country where they flew. CF-HAS was burnt by vandals whilst 'HTM, the ex-British civil machine, actually returned in May 1958 for use by Dan-Air but was damaged beyond repair at Luqa, Malta on the 20th of that month.

Skyways last York, G-AGNV, ex-TS798, used on cargo flights for Pan American World Airways until 1964, was once displayed in the Skyfame Museum at Staverton in Gloucestershire and is now with the Royal Air Force Museum, displayed at Cosford Aerospace Museum.

The only major variant was the first prototype re-engined with Bristol Hercules VI engines as in the Lancaster B Mk II and the only York C Mk 2. Although successful, no major performance improvements were made despite the slight extra power (30 more to 1,650 hp) probably because drag was increased and, with sufficient Merlins available, the variant was not proceeded with. The only other external variants were 'Ascalon' with its square windows and the only Canadian Victory-built York, FM400, with built-up floor and windows parallel to the ground line.

The York's fuselage, 78 feet 6 inches long, is a semi-monocoque structure approximately square in cross-section, built in five sections. Vertical frames and formers, with horizontal stringers and flush riveted skin make up the shell. The 21-seat version had seats arranged three abreast, six in the forward cabin, 15 aft, cloakrooms and toilets opposite the main entrance door between the cabins, and galley and baggage space at the back. Both cabins had emergency exits in the roof.

The interior of a passenger-carrying York, with 'Star Girl'.

Chapter Nine

Preserved Lancs and Yorks

From a total production of 7,377 Lancasters, 18 are still in existence, 38 years after the first prototype flew in 1941. At present only three are potentially airworthy with much effort being expended to get them back into their element.

The Royal Air Force's Battle of Britain Memorial Flight, besides its Spitfires and Hurricanes, maintains an airworthy Lancaster, PA474, an ex-PR I built by Vickers Armstrong at Chester in 1945 for use by the 'Tiger' force. It was converted for photo survey and used by No 82 Squadron in Africa and Western Germany. Loaned to Flight Refuelling in August 1952 for trials, it was transferred to Cranfield for Aeronautical research in 1954. With an aerofoil section mounted on top of its specially strengthened fuselage, it became a flying laboratory, one wing tested being that of a Folland Midge. Handley Page received a research contract to carry out trials of a Midge wing equipped with suction for boundary layer control mounted on Cranfield's Lancaster but it was found more economic to make a half wing from scratch. With 45° leading edge sweep, 8 feet 4 inches root chord, 5 feet 8 inches tip chord, it was 13 feet tall and two Budworth gas-turbines of 60 hp were installed in the Lanc to provide the required suction. The first flight was made on October 2 1962 and the trials continued until late in 1963. Flown to Waddington in August 1965, via Wroughton and Henlow, it was refurbished as KM-B, Squadron Leader Nettleton's aircraft for the daylight raid on Augsburg on August 17 1942.

This Lancaster has been seen by millions of people, having regularly taken part in many air displays and flypasts, both at home and on the continent. Regrettably, because it required major wing repairs, it was grounded at Coningsby during 1978 but should be back in the air by Easter of 1979—long may she fly!

The UKs other flying Lancaster belongs to the Strathallan Aircraft Collection and was purchased in Canada. Built by Victory Aircraft at Malton in 1945, as KB976, it joined No 405 Squadron at Linton-on-Ouse in 1945. It was converted for maritime reconnaissance duties until its retirement on April 9 1964 when it became CF-TQC, a water bomber, until 1969 when it was grounded, to be purchased by Sir William Roberts in 1974. It was prepared for its Atlantic ferry flight by Strathallan's engineer and left Edmonton International Airport on May 16 1975 for Glasgow via Toronto, Halifax, Gander and Iceland.

Spirit of Caledonia, now registered G-BCOH, arrived safely at Strathallan on June 11 and low priority refurbishing has been in progress ever since. Turrets will be re-fitted and the next flight could be in 1979!

The third Lancaster should have flown in Canada by the time this is read as major efforts have been made by the Canadian Warplane Heritage to rebuild FM213 at Skyharbour Airport, Ontario. Originally converted to 10MR format, it was later rebuilt as a Mk 10SR and served with No 107 (Rescue) Unit, Torbay, Newfoundland before being mounted on a pylon at Goderich as a tribute to BCATPs 12 EFTSs. All the Merlins have been removed and overhauled, systems have been overhauled and replaced where necessary, so, providing the MOT requirements can be met, the Lanc will be flown to Mount Hope to join the rest of the CWH collection and restored in Bomber Command colours.

Two more Lancasters are displayed in England, the famous 'S' for Sugar in the Royal Air Force Museum at Hendon and the unlucky G-ASXX (ex-NX611 and WU15) now at Scampton's main gate. Both have had a book written about them (see Bibliography) so a few words will suffice. 'Sugar', perhaps too beautifully painted and factory fresh, carries 137 bombs painted on her nose although her log lists 138 raids, 70 with No 83 Squadron as 'Queenie' (OL-Q) and 68 with No 467 (RAAF) Squadron, coded PO-S. Despite flying over 800 hours on ops, and dropping over 500 tons of bombs, she was earmarked for 'Tiger' Force after VE Day, moving from Waddington, her last operational base, to Metheringham to prepare for her trip to Okinawa.

However, within a week, R5868 had been allocated to No 15 Maintenance Unit at Wroughton as non-effective equipment, but is believed to have gone into storage at Fulbeck for the Historical Aircraft Collection. She was rescued by Scampton's station commander in the spring of 1959 for static display on May 14 when No 617 Squadron received its standard, and was then sited opposite the guardroom, still coded PO-S. This was later to be changed back to OL-Q by No 83 Squadron, flying its Vulcans from Scampton.

In 1970 she was selected for the RAF Museum instead of the then airworthy PA474 and moved to No 71 MU at Bicester for refurbishing before being installed at Hendon on March 12 1972, and so beautifully painted. Here 'Sugar' rests proudly for all time, surrounded by a selection of weapons which the Lancaster could have carried.

Taking her place at Scampton is NX611, bearing the codes of their station flight, YF-C, on long-term loan to the Royal Air Force by Lord Lilford, well maintained and

HAPS G-ASXX leaves Australia.

regularly painted. This Mk VII was built by Austin Motors at Longbridge in 1945, the first of 150 finished to Far East specification for 'Tiger' Force. Unused, she was stored at Llandow until allocated to the French order in 1952 when she was moved to Woodford for modification to MR standard. The Martin electric mid-upper turret was removed, ASV radar was fitted, as were the two rear observation windows and gear for carrying an airborne lifeboat. WU-15, now dark blue all over, joined L'Aeronavale and served in France and North Africa. Overhauled at Le Bourget in 1962 with a much harder wearing white finish, she was flown to Noumea in New Caledonia to serve for two more years when she was donated to the Historic Aircraft Preservation Society and flown to Bankstown, near Sydney, in August 1964. Here she received much careful attention and funds were raised to cover certification and the flight home.

Leaving Mascot on April 25 1965, G-ASXX flew the 12,000 miles in 70 hours, arriving at Biggin Hill on May 13 in time for that year's Air Fair. The journey had been reasonably trouble free and she had, by then, flown 2,411 hours! One engine and propeller were out of hours but she was maintained regularly and repainted in Bomber Command colours as HA-P (218 Squadron). After much hard work she was ready for her first outing—to Scampton for the 24th anniversary of the Dams raid on May 19/20! She was flown by the late Flt Lt Neil Williams, then an RAF test pilot and already an international aerobatic champion, who was to captain her on all her flights.

With the demise of HAPS, she was taken over by Reflectaire Ltd and successfully flown to Lavenham in Suffolk, Hullavington in Wiltshire (where she was re-painted and re-coded GL-C, the initials of Leonard Cheshire) and then Blackpool where she arrived on June 26 1970, a sad day for her last flight. Here she languished for two winters, suffering at the hands of the weather, to become Lot 63 at a winding-up auction on April 29 1972. Unsold, she was purchased in a private deal by Lord Lilford two days later. Another winter was to pass before

NX611 was to move to her present home in August 1973, on board six Queen Mary trailers after a difficult dismantling by RAF volunteers in atrocious weather! She was completely stripped, corrosion removed, and repaired before being finally erected and handed over on May 17 1974, at a ceremony ending in a flypast by PA474, then based at nearby Waddington.

Two other ex-French Navy Mk VII Lancasters are preserved in Australia and New Zealand. NX622, later WU-16, was presented to the Air Force Association, Perth, in 1963, and re-camouflaged by No 25 Squadron, Citizen Air Force. It is coded CA-F on its port side and AF-C on the starboard, the latter for the Australian Flying Corps. At Auckland, New Zealand, the Museum of Transport and Technology, Western Springs, proudly displays NX665, disguised as ND752, AA-O of No 75 (NZ) Squadron on its starboard side, with PB457, SR-V of 101 Squadron on its port side. Like NX611, it came from storage at No 38 MU, and flew with L'Aeronavale as WU-13 from 1951 to 1964 when it ended its life in New Caledonia from where it was presented to the 'Kiwis' who served with Bomber Command.

Also in Australia is a real Lancaster, a Mk 1, W4783, displayed inside at the Australian War Museum, Canberra. One of only two Lancasters sent to Australia during the war, it was allocated A66-2 but still bears its original squadron codes, AR-G, of 460 Squadron, Binbrook, Lincolnshire. It flew 90 ops before flying home in 1944 for a War Bonds drive—donors or purchasers of bonds to the value of over £A100 were given a free flight!

All the other preserved Lancasters are Canadian built Mk Xs, surprisingly all in their home country! KB944 is displayed at Rockcliffe Air Station, North Ottawa, by the National Museum of Science and Technology, with codes NA-P (428 Squadron). It flew to England at the end of war but no operations are recorded. Returning home, it was stored till January 1955, when it was used at Greenwood, Nova Scotia, until 1957, before allocation for the then RCAF Museum.

A magnificent specimen, converted as a Mk 10AR,

Four interior shots of KB944: **Above** *Cockpit.* **Left** *Radio compartment.* **Bottom** *Looking forward with mid-upper turret base and ammunition feeds.* **Below** *Looking aft with that essential item!* (G.L. Marshall).

Above *KB839 at Greenwood, Nova Scotia* (G.L. Marshall).

Below *FM159 at Nanton, Alberta* (Ian M. Macdonald).

with lengthened nose, is displayed at Greenwood, Nova Scotia, but internally it has been stripped out. KB839 served with No 408 Squadron flying from Rockcliffe.

FM136, coded VN-N, is displayed on a pylon at McCall Field, Calgary, Alberta, having been used by 407 Squadron, Comox, for Maritime Patrol and disposed of to the Lancaster Club in 1961.

FM159, another Mk 10MP, was bought by Mr George White, Nanton, Alberta, on October 4 1960. Vandal-proofed, it is hoped, with cockpit and turret glazing covered by a protective layer of aluminium sheeting, bearing codes RX-159 on its non-standard glossy black paint, it is mounted in flying attitude in a park. Another long nosed Mk 10AR, once a B Mk X serving with No 428 Squadron at Middleton St George, KB882 was used by No 408 Squadron and is on display at St Jacques Airport, Edmunston, New Brunswick, belonging to the local Air Cadet Squadron.

FM212, incorrectly coded CF-S, a Mk 10P used by No 9 Transport Group and 408 Squadron at Rockcliffe, is displayed in the Jackson Park Sunken Gardens at Windsor, Ontario, whilst FM104, once displayed in Toronto's Canadian National Exhibition Grounds, Ontario Park, has not been reported lately.

KB889, another Maritime Patrol modification, owned by Mr K. Shortt, is being worked on at Oshawa Airport, Ontario, with the hoped-for intention of flying again one day. Victor Leonhardt, now living at Westerose in Alberta, purchased two Lancasters from Penhold Air Force Base through the War Assets Corporation in 1947. They were KB944, coded EQ-K, and KB941 (PT-U). The fuselage of the former still resides in a thicket at Pidgeon Lake, but Mr. Leonhardt took the latter with him when he moved from Drumhiller and presumably it still exists.

Two cockpits are displayed, that of DV372, ex-467 (RAAF) Squadron in the Imperial War Museum, London and that of KB848, one of the Mk 10DC (Drone Carriers) is in the Canadian National Aviation Collection, whilst the shot-up hulk of another, unidentified but for a plate in the cockpit bearing 41/372, is on Shilo artillery range in Manitoba! The Western Canadian Aviation Museum hopes to obtain the cockpit section of this.

All the Manchesters have gone, even an intact Vulture engine is unknown, but two Yorks are preserved, one at Cosford Aerospace Museum. This is G-AGNV, once displayed at the Skyfame Museum, Staverton, as LV633. It has been painstakingly rebuilt by technicians at RAF Cosford. The second York is at Lasham, the home of Dan-Air. G-ANTK was the last York flown by them, earlier used by the RAF as MW232 on the Berlin airlift and cargo flights to the Woomera rocket range in Australia. It had been presented to local Scouts as a bunkhouse, the fuselage top being covered with roofing felt to make it waterproof! The Scouts were given a Comet in exchange and the York is in process of being rebuilt by members of the Dan-Air Preservation Society for static display.

Luckily, the enthusiast and aircraft modeller has a variety of Lancasters to study and, we hope, see flying for many years to come.

Chapter Ten

The Manchester

The 'Lanc' is one of the most popular aircraft as a modelling subject and there are now several quite good kits available from which you can choose your own particular favourite. In spite of this there are many variants not available in kit form and these make interesting conversion projects for the more ambitious modeller. My part in this book is to show how some of these can be improvised from the kits available and to suggest ways of displaying the finished model. I also cover possible variants of some of the conversions.

I hope that we have come up with a few less familiar shapes for you to model as well as some of the more popular ones and that we have extended your knowledge of the aircraft, in particular of its test-bed and 'odd ball' uses.

The kits available at the time of writing are the B1 from Airfix, the Mk I and the Dam Buster from Revell in 1:72 scale and a B1 from Novo in 1:96 scale. My especial thanks to these manufacturers for supplying samples of their products for me to use. There may also still be

available, in some model shops, the Frog version which is particularly useful as it has the bulged bomb bay doors of the Mk III capable of accommodating the 12,000 lb bomb. None of these kits, unfortunately, includes an H_2S underfuselage blister. Of course, the Frog kit is not available at the moment but these old Frog moulds have a habit of turning up under another label and it is possible that this may happen again.

Tamiya is the only manufacturer to produce a Lancaster in 1:48 scale, in fact they do us proud with two basic versions, the B1/III and the B1 special in Dam Buster or Grand Slam variants. However, the Lancaster story is a lot broader than that covered by these kits and here the specialist vacform producers, like Gordon Sutcliffe the maker of Contrail kits, help out with conversion parts for some variants. Again many thanks to Gordon for his help.

You will see from the photographs of my models in construction that in some instances I used Revell, in others Airfix parts, but either make will do equally well—it just happens that the Airfix kit has fixed bomb bay doors but a more-difficult-to-alter top deck and Revell has openable doors and an easier top deck. All kits have a row of 'windows' and lots of rivets which need filling and sanding down respectively. The Airfix wingtips need reshaping to the more elliptical plan of the accompanying drawing. The Airfix kits were temporarily out of stock at the time of writing, the master moulds being in for refurbishing, and the parts I used were factory test shots and may therefore show more filling than would be necessary with an off-the-shelf kit.

This is not a book of basic modelling techniques and I will assume that you will be doing test assemblies at each stage and that any adjustments and rectifications will be done automatically, especially along the fuselage centreline join, engine nacelle fitting and wing and tailplane leading and trailing edges.

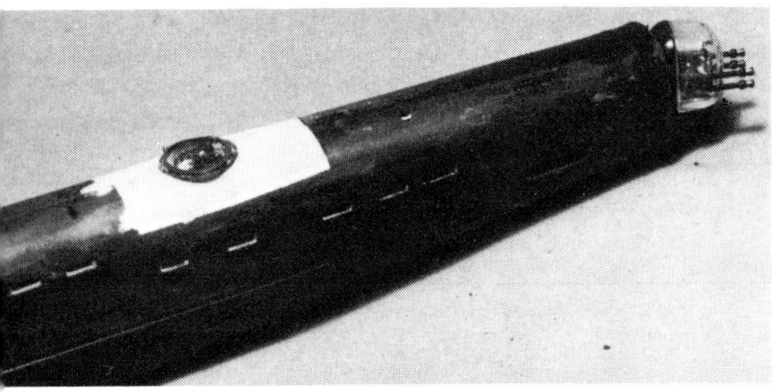

Above *The top of a fuselage filled to accept a new turret.*

Below *Contrail Vac-form wing halves are rough cut ready for sanding.*

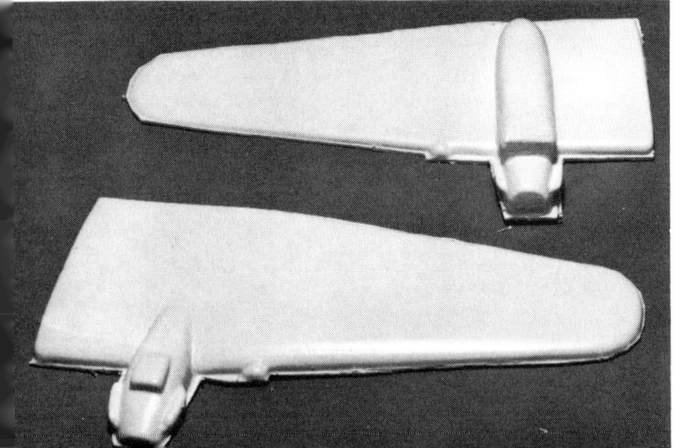

Manchester and prototype Lancasters

The Manchester first prototype L7246 was not, during its early flights, fitted with the central fixed fin. The second prototype and production Manchesters had the fixed fin and small fin-rudder assemblies. The Mk IA was fitted with enlarged fin and rudder assemblies and the central fin was deleted. Thus we already have several basic Manchester types which we can summarise thus:

1   First prototype L7246 with small twin fins and

rudders—no turrets. 80 feet 2 inches span. 28 foot span tail.

2 Modified first prototype L7247 and second prototype with additions of central fixed fin—nose and tail turrets.

3 Production versions with dorsal turret 90 feet 1 inch span. 28 foot span tail.

4 Production version without dorsal turret 90 feet 1 inch span. 28 foot span tail.

5 Modified to Mk IA with what were to become standard Lancaster-type larger twin fins and rudders and 33 foot span tail.

The last of these alternatives is obviously the simplest as it is the nearest to any kit Lancaster available and any alterations will be confined to the wing and engine units. Any of the Lancaster kits can be used, the Revell being the easiest to fit with a dorsal turret as it already has the aperture in the correct place, but the rear of the fuselage will have to be altered to remove the fairings in front of the rear turret. This is a lot easier to do on the Airfix kit as these are not so pronounced. None of the 1:72 scale kits has really got the correct shaped turrets but, as you will find if you try to mould your own, this is technically very dodgy unless you try to do it in two halves. However, installed in the model the kit offerings do not look too bad. The Airfix fuselage top turret fairing should be removed and scrap plastic-card cemented inside as a base to which filler may be applied if making one of the types without the dorsal turret. For further details of this refer to the later conversion to a Lancastrian.

The dorsal turret will have to be moulded, of course, and this should present few problems as it is a nice easy shape. A short length of $\frac{5}{8}$ in wooden dowel can be used

with the shape of the turret carved and shaped carefully on one end slightly undersize to the shape shown on the drawings. This is used as a former to mould the turret in clear plastic card. Most modellers will be familiar with the method but for those who are not, cut out a clearance hole through which this former will pass easily, with an equal gap of, say, 20 thou all round, in a sheet of plywood 6 in square. The clear plastic sheet is pinned over this hole and heated over a cooker ring until soft, at which stage smoothly and firmly push the former through to the required depth. Hold it until cool and finally plunge it into cold water to set the shape. Un-pin and remove it from the plywood and trim off the surplus to leave, we hope, a nice clear new turret.

The fuselage can now be assembled with all interior detail, crew if you require them and, for the Airfix kit, narrow strips of clear plastic inside the rows of windows. The next stage is to modify the kit wings and, as you will see from the drawings (see front endpaper), this can be done by removing sections from the outer mainplanes, alternating upper and lower surfaces. This gives an overlap to the parts, and results in a stepped leading edge when all the parts are re-assembled, which can be filed to shape, filling a bit as necessary. Take care that the wings are assembled free from warp and are true and level.

The engines should now be built up to the mainplanes and there are several ways in which this can be accomplished. The first method I would suggest is to use the inner nacelles from the kit as a basis on which to work. Cut off the front of each nacelle half and then build up between the undersurface of the wing and the nacelle with scrap plastic card to give a deeper 'belly' to the nacelle rear.

Wingtip modification.

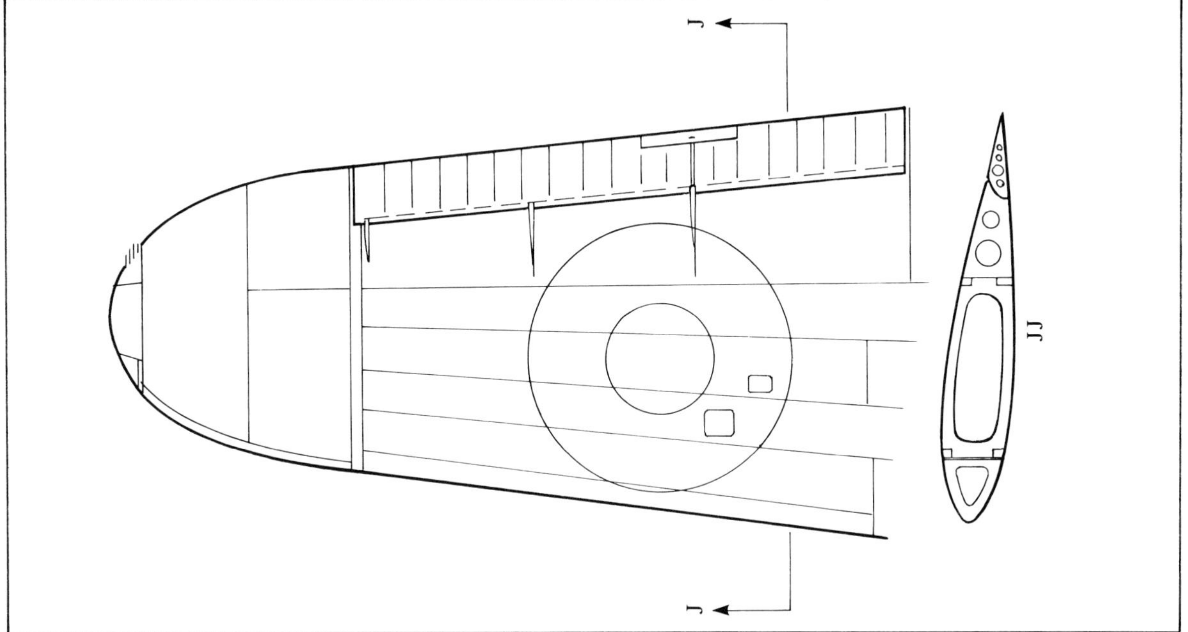

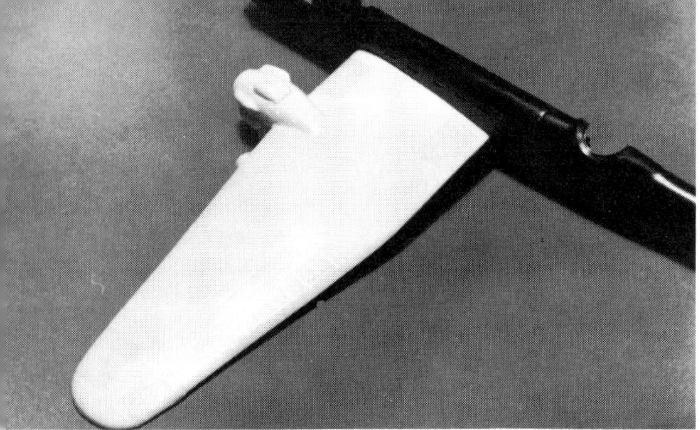

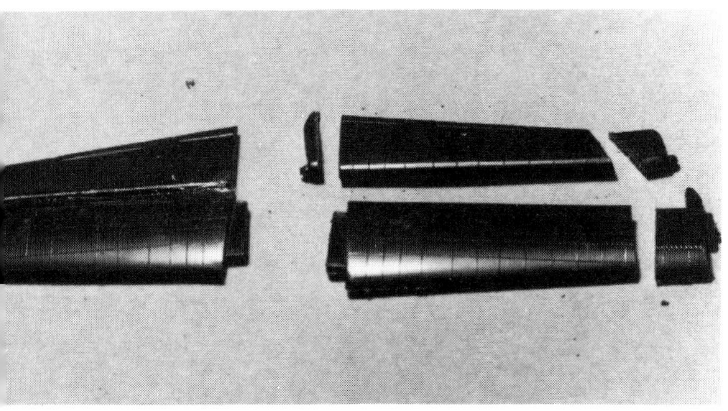

To reduce the length of the nacelle, first cut out a section approximately $4\frac{1}{2}$ mm wide and also cut off the bottom panels. When the two modified parts are cemented together the underside is sheeted over with scrap plastic card and then the units are fitted up to the underside of the wing. Score heavily with a sharp point and build up the main shape with Plastic Padding or similar filler and, when dry, file to the correct shape and size. The airscoops and exhaust stacks can then be added to finalise the new cowling shape. The propeller blades will require slight trimming to reduce the overall diameter and the undercarriage doors will also require trimming as they are a little shorter than the Lancaster's. Cut two small pieces off each end and cement these offcuts to the underside of the nacelles, fairing in with body filler.

If you like working in wood then the new front cowlings can be carved from suitable blocks of hard balsa, sanded smooth and filled with a coat or two of dope in which has been mixed a little talcum powder. Alternatively carve undersize and use the resulting former to mould two new cowlings from plastic card. Do each engine in two halves, left and right, as the kit parts are moulded.

Gordon Sutcliffe's Contrail kits take some of the heat out of the Manchester conversion by providing a sheet of vacuum moulded parts for the wing, engine units, triple tail fins and the dorsal turret. I suggest that this might be a useful way of attempting this conversion.

My particular model is a hybrid, with the Airfix fuselage, Contrail wings and engine units, Frog undercarriage and door unit, and modified Airfix tailplane.

The Contrail wing units are, of course, the main parts that concern us and I found my Precision Petite mini power-drill equipped with a cutting disc ideal for removing the main parts from the carrier sheet. This type of small 12 volt drill is perhaps one of the best investments the serious scratchbuilder or converter can make, although its use does require practice to avoid unfortunate mistakes. The same cutting disc can be used to grind away a lot of the spare material before the final sanding is done.

A sheet of wet-and-dry paper, fixed to an offcut of hardboard with masking tape, provides a useful base on which to finish off the smoothing and working down of the two surfaces of upper and lower wing halves which have to be joined. Keep the wet-and-dry paper clean and wet—but not running with water—you will learn to judge it by experience.

Before joining the upper and lower halves of each wing together, you may decide to remove the moulded 'exhausts', as I did, and to replace them with shaped scraps of sprue. Cut the exhausts off and cement scrap strips of plastic card inside the nacelles and, when dry, fill on the outside with body putty and smooth to shape. Cut eight identical new exhausts and cement in place as shown on the drawings. You may also at this stage like to open out the air inlet apertures on the cowling front and top, again backing these with scrap plastic on the insides to represent radiator, etc. If you are removing the undercarriage doors this can be done without too much

The finished model of a Manchester ZN-V in its final form. Note the code letters which have been painted free hand.

trouble after the wings are completed. To use the Airfix undercarriage you will have to insert a sheet of 30 thou plastic card on which to mount the main legs, etc, to the inside of the nacelle, and this must be done before the wing halves are joined. The Frog kit has separate parts for undercarriage doors in the open position, complete with mountings for the legs and retraction rams and linkage. This assembly fits very neatly to the Contrail nacelles.

Do a trial assembly of the wings using Sellotape to hold the parts together and check that the wing root will fit into the cut-outs in the sides of the Airfix fuselage. You will have to trim a slice off the root to obtain the correct span but that is best done after the wing halves are joined. All being well, cement the two pairs of wing halves together and, when dry, cut along the line just outboard of the nacelles and, with a file, adjust the abutting joints to give the correct dihedral angle to the outer planes. Re-cement together and leave to dry well propped up at the correct angle. Fill and finish as necessary when dry.

Meanwhile the Airfix kit tailplane can be re-cut to the shorter span of the Manchester, the fin/rudder assemblies re-shaped and you can either use the central fin from the Contrail kit or build one from plastic card.

That, roughly, is all the major work that needs to be done, the rest is final assembly, detailing and painting. Then you will have a replica of the ancestor of probably the most famous bomber of all time.

Chapter Eleven

Conversions to other Marks

To follow the Lancaster story through in model form we can now consider some alterations to other Marks. Again we can use almost any of the kits from Revell, Airfix, Novo or even Tamiya. My suggestions are mostly for the 1:72 scale kits as these must have more appeal to the average aircraft modeller.

Following the simpler conversions I shall go into the possibilities of extending the story to the Lancastrian and the York, which were essentially, though not wholly, civil versions.

Lancaster Mk II

The Mark II Lancaster is, of course, fitted with Bristol Hercules radial air-cooled engines of which just over 300 were produced. Most were fitted with the three turrets of the standard Lancaster but some had the FN64 under-turret fitted as, of course, did some Mk 1/IIIs.

Later aircraft and those in for repair were fitted with bulged bomb doors and one, LL735, was used to test the Metrovick F2/4 jet engine in the rear. This had a faired-in front turret, as did the Lancaster Python test-bed described later, but the rear of the fuselage accommodated the F2/4 with a large air intake on top of the fuselage and no top turret.

Any of the 1:72 scale Lancaster kits can be used for this conversion and details of modification to the Airfix kit are described in *Airfix Magazine Annual No 8*. The Revell kit is particularly useful in that it has the bomb doors as a separate part and this saves having to cut it away in order to fit bulged doors, as required for the Airfix kit. The Revell kit also has an aperture for the ventral turret which is available from the Revell Dam Buster kit or can be made simply from scrap.

All we need to do therefore is to mate the radial engines (see drawing at top of page 36) from a Halifax to the rear nacelles of a Lancaster which has had its Merlins amputated. The drill is to separate slightly the nacelle fronts by about an $\frac{1}{8}$ in using a wedge of scrap plastic, and then to build up and fair in to a circular section, with Plastic Padding, to accept the radials. You can always use a couple of the Merlins to make a Merlin engined Beaufighter.

An alternative to moulding new bomb bay doors is to build up underneath the kit originals, again with Plastic Padding, but do always remember with this material to score well the surface to which it is to be attached and seal it with a coat of thin varnish as it is slightly porous.

Lancaster Mk VI

Really the Mk VI was a test-bed for the 1,635 hp two stage Merlin but some six or seven saw service with operational squadrons. It led, of course, to the larger-spanned Lincoln which, although just outside the scope of this book, was a link in the chain, started with the Manchester and ended with the Shackleton.

The easiest way to do this conversion is to take the engine parts from a Frog Shackleton but this kit is not readily available, however, if you do have a scrap one spare anywhere, then give it a new lease of life by using its bits for this conversion.

Whichever basic 1:72 scale Lancaster kit you use, you must fill in the side windows and the top turret position as described for the Lancastrian. Some of the Mark VIs had a faired-over front turret as also mentioned for the Python test-bed. An H_2S radar scanner fairing is fitted underneath the fuselage and it is worth while moulding this from clear plastic. First carve it slightly undersize from a close grained wood and then mould it as previously described. It is a good idea to do several as there are many variants of the Lancaster fitted with this H_2S and there is no kit, apart from the Tamiya 1:48 scale, that has this feature.

To return to the engines, which are the main alteration, I will assume that you have not got a spare Shackleton and we must therefore explore the alternatives. You could carve them from wood, of course, but I would suggest that one only is carved and used as a mould for all four. The rear of the nacelles can be built up using the basic kit parts and the conversion is then very similar to that for the Mk II. Mould your cowlings in three parts, port and starboard sides and a front. These are then united to a bulkhead just behind the front to which you can build up the radiator detail. By far the simplest way is to use one of the Contrail kits, those for the Lincoln (which really does

Completed model of a Lancastrian.

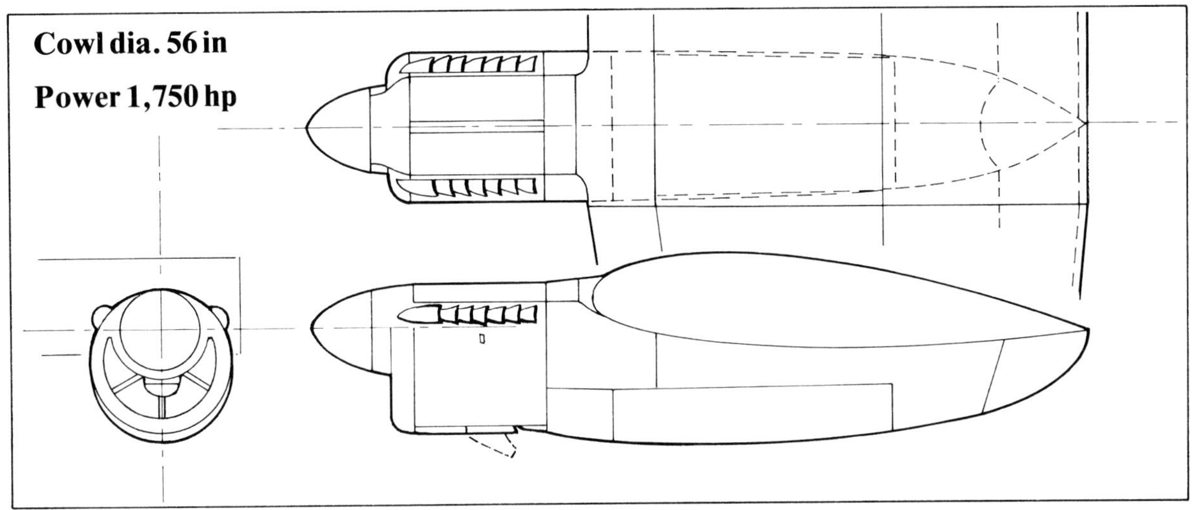

Merlin 85 Power Egg—Lancaster VI.

carry on the line of the Avro heavies) or the Avro 688 Tudor. Careful construction and filling where required will then provide you with the four engines you need to do this unusual Lancaster conversion.

An even more 'odd ball' version is the ND 784, the Mamba test-bed used by Armstrong Siddeley. There are not many five engined aircraft that you can model so if your inclination is for the unique then I offer that as a suggestion.

Air Sea Rescue Lancaster

The use of the Lancaster for ASR duties is not as well publicised as its, perhaps more glamorous, bombing escapades but it nevertheless performed valuable service in this role. Coastal Command used such Lancasters, as did Canada, and many were used on photographic reconnaissance and survey duties.

ASR Lancasters were fitted with an airborne lifeboat, a similar conversion to that carried out on Warwicks, which was carried under the bomb doors. It was of rather shallow draught but an inflatable canopy and sides made it particularly seaworthy. It was fitted with sails, masts and spars, supplies of fuel and water, rations, flares and full emergency kits. It was, of course, dropped by parachutes and the carrying aircraft were fitted with radar aids and the bulged underbelly housing.

To model this particular variant is relatively simple as it is virtually a standard Lancaster but without the upper turret. For my model I chose the Revell kit as it is intended to be displayed making a low pass over a ditched pilot, with flaps down and boat ready to go on the next pass. I may even include a ditched aircraft in the sea but am still looking for records of an actual 'happening'.

The lifeboat can be carved from wood or moulded in plastic card, in fact any of the usual options can be used. Have you thought of trying papier mâché? This is very simple if you use Plasticine to shape the boat, easy to get it to fit up to the bomb doors but form it slightly undersize. Cover the Plasticine shape with tissue paper soaked in flour-and-water paste or Polycell (wallpaper hanging paste) applying several layers. Leave to dry, in an airing cupboard is ideal and, when completely hard, peel the Plasticine out and apply a coat or two of model aircraft dope with a little talcum powder mixed in as a filler. This technique produces a tough shell, in fact, where all else fails, it can even be used for engine nacelles and is a method not to be ignored just because some may consider it childish. It is not only taught in most infant schools, at one time it was in vogue for decorative furniture, trays, boxes, etc, and these are now expensive antiques.

The radar bulge must be carved from wood and moulded in clear plastic sheet. The shape and location is shown in the drawings and should present no problems as it really is one of the simplest shapes to make.

With the kits now available it should be possible to produce every version of the Lancaster and the Manchester, although some will require the extensive modifications referred to while others need only a small amount of work. There are other one-offs like the tanker (of which two were produced), further test-beds and experimentals, even civil versions. I was told that Lancasters were used as agricultural contract aircraft for aerial application of fertilisers in Australia but I have

A moulded radar blister has now been fitted and the model is given a white undercoat (see also drawing on page 37).

Above Nose profile formers have been fitted ready for application of the filler. Note the heavy scoring to all parts.

Below Plastic Padding filler has been applied and is filed and sanded to shape.

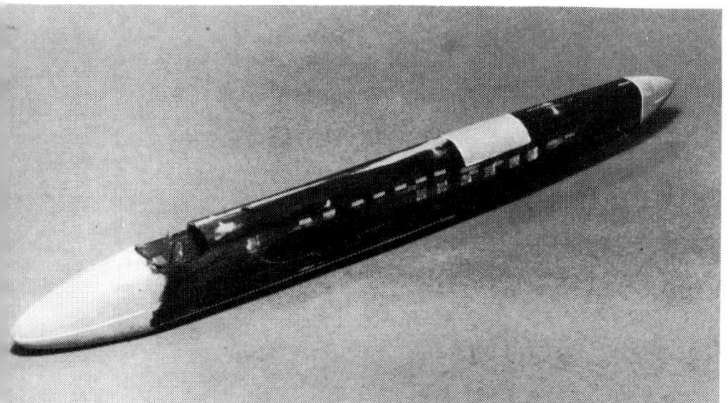

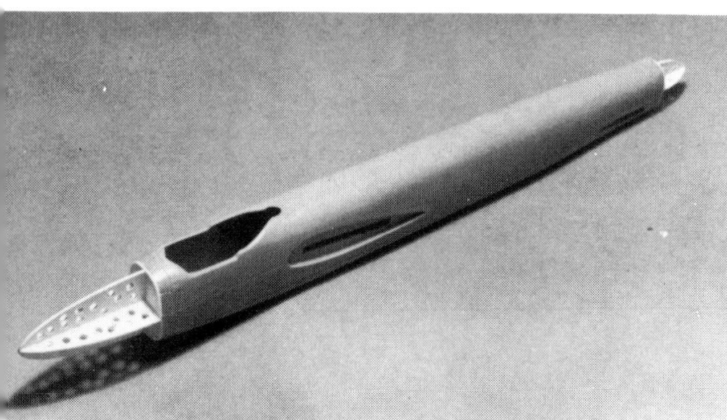

Above A Novo kit with the nose and tail profile formers in place. The rear turret position requires very little filler.

Below A Lancastrian in its final silver livery with black registration letters. Note the re-shaped rudder.

never seen pictures of these in action and such a use seems most unlikely. Nevertheless, there must be many unusual uses for the old warhorse and it remains a fascinating subject of further research for any dedicated Lancaster fan and I hope that we have given you some ideas and opened up the field for further models using the techniques described.

Avro Lancastrian

This, I think, is one of the most attractive of Lancaster conversions and is also one which requires no parts that are not in every Lancaster kit. It is a streamlined Lancaster with a new nose and tail end to replace the turrets of the military version.

I again used an Airfix kit for no other reason than that I prefer the undercarriage and the bomb doors are integral mouldings.

First, the fuselage. Cement strips of plastic card behind the 'window' apertures and fill them in to present a smooth outside surface. Cut new square windows as shown on the drawings on pages 60, 62 and 63–drill four holes and cut out roughly finishing off with a small square section file. Cement strips of clear plastic card behind the new windows and apply Humbrol or something similar. Mask as a protection during subsequent work and also for painting or spraying. Cut away the top turret fairing or a rectangular section out of the top of each fuselage half and then cement the fuselage together, including any extra cockpit detailing such as crew, etc, that you decide on.

Cut off the nose and tail at the points shown on the photographs of my model in construction. If you like using wood then there is no reason why the nose and tail fairings cannot be carved from suitable blocks and cemented in place. If you get the impression that I do not like using wood on a plastic model—then you are right!

My method, which is clearly shown in the photographs, is to cut out from 30 thou plastic card the shape of the side view of the new nose, and also the plan view which is cut in half down the centre line. These are cemented together to form a cross and in turn cemented to a bulkhead on the cut-off fuselage nose. I drilled plenty of holes and scored the parts well, as a key for the filler, before assembly. It would probably be better to part fill the four nose segments with scrap plastic parts to save on filler, but anyway the basic idea is to build up the streamlined shape with Plastic Padding. When dry it is simple to carve and file to shape, finishing being done with wet-and-dry (used wet) wrapped around a block of wood. Of course, the tail fairing is made in a similar manner to the nose.

The upper turret location is blanked off with a rectangle of plastic card and two-part bulkheads front and rear, the whole being filled with Plastic Padding and filed to the line and section of the fuselage. Useful stuff, Plastic Padding, especially for filling large areas, but you must score the plastic well for it to get a grip. The only snag is that it tends to get air bubbles but where these show they can be filled with Green Stuff or other body putty.

The next step is just kit assembly of the remainder of

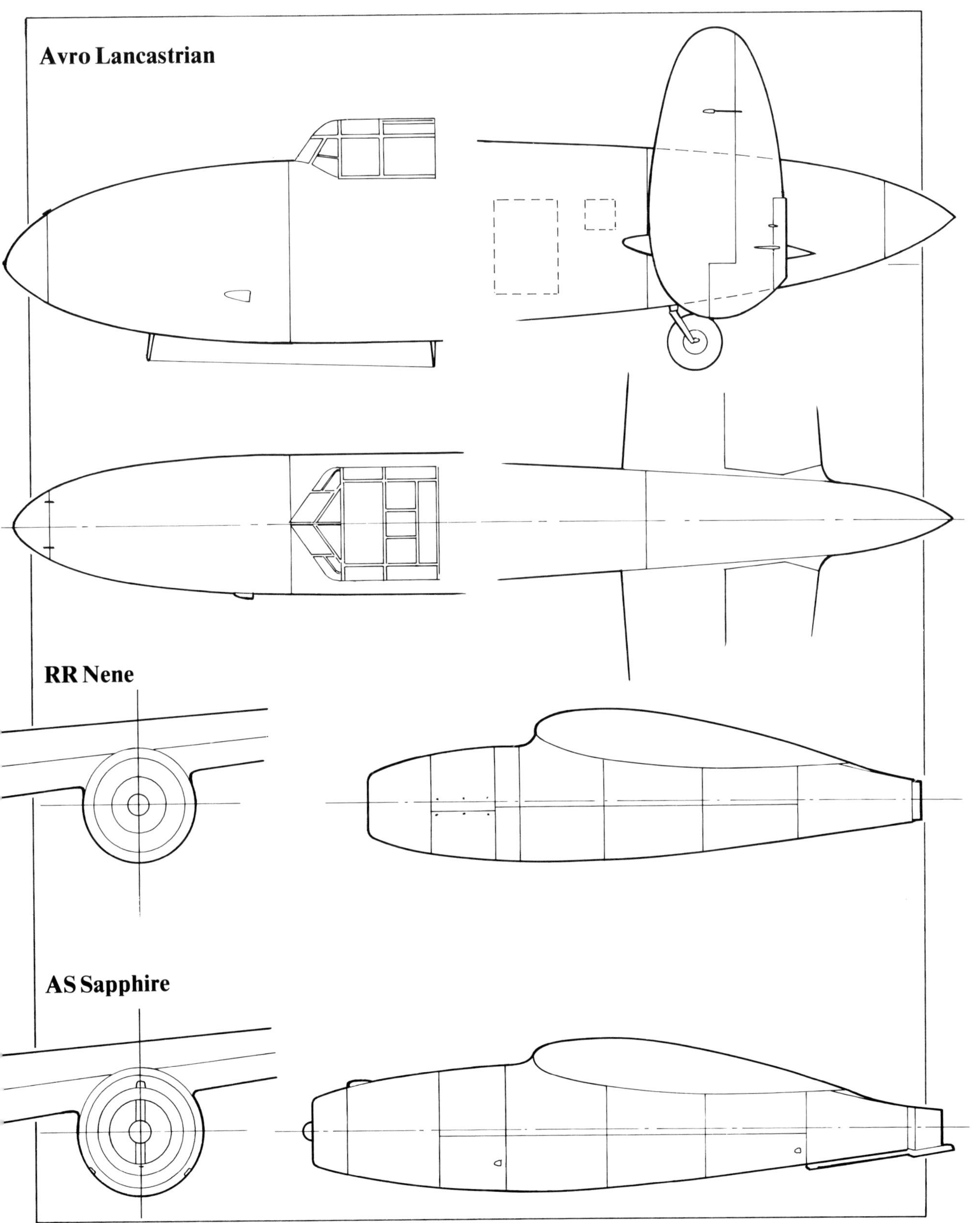

Avro Lancastrian
RR Nene
AS Sapphire

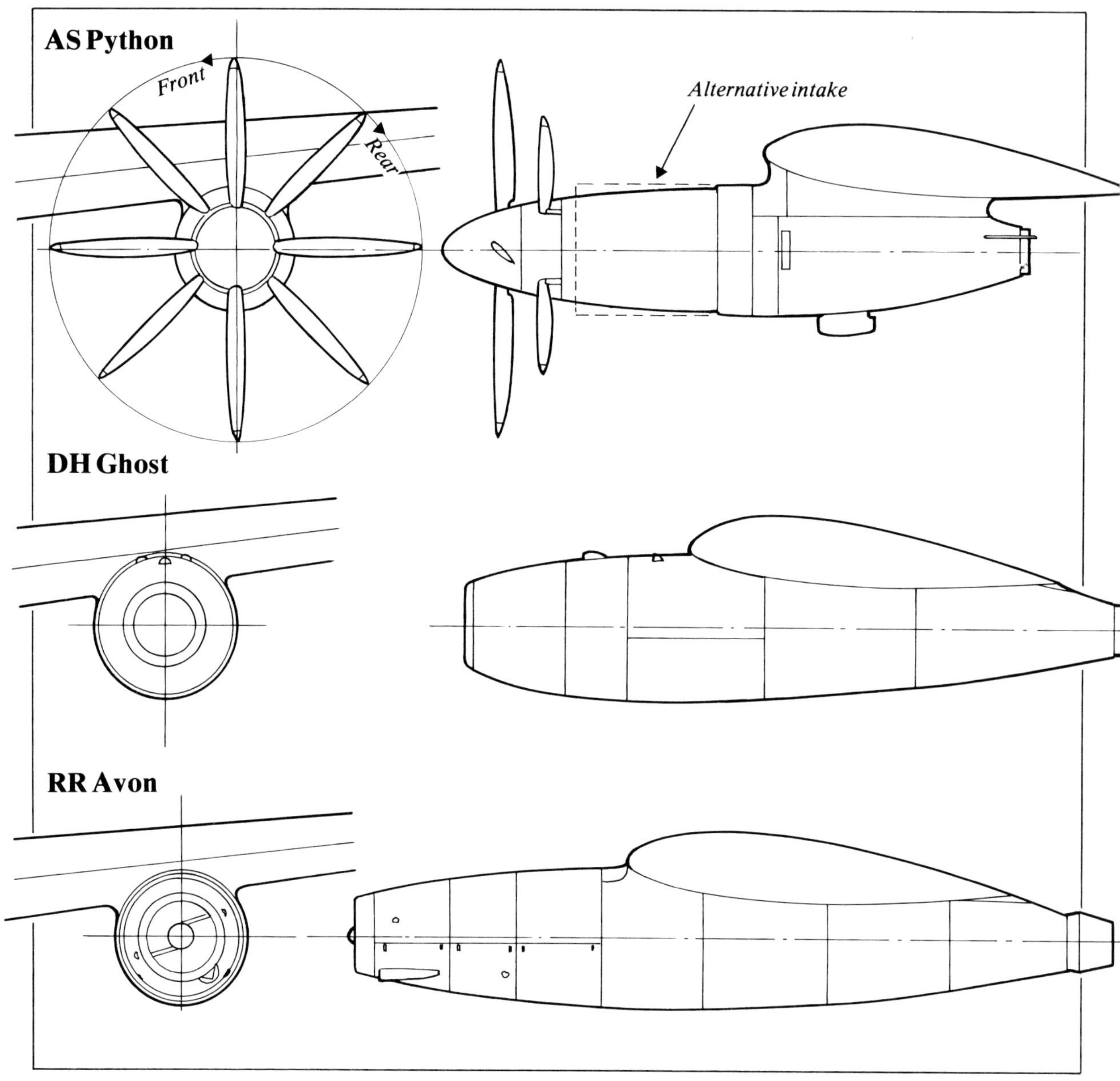

the parts, wings, engine, undercarriage, tailplane, etc, with the exception of the rudders on some aircraft which you will see are slightly modified. Note the new shape as on the drawings and photographs which can easily be altered on the model. Just cut out a quarter circle from the bottom of the trailing edge, cement in a rectangle of plastic card and file and sand to the new shape.

Lancastrian test-beds

Having made the basic Lancastrian there are yet further members of the family that can be attempted and, of course, these have been well described and documented in the first part of the book.

I chose the Nene test-bed although the Avon and Sapphire are all similar. As a basis for my model I used the Novo 1:96 scale Lancaster and it is probably a good idea for younger modellers also to try their hands at a simple conversion of an inexpensive kit.

As a start, carve away the upper turret fairings—only a small amount of filler is required and this should first be applied inside the fuselage. File to roughly the correct shape and apply further filler to the outside and, when dry, use wet-and-dry round a block of wood to shape to the rest of the fuselage. Add any cockpit detail you require—there is none in the kit but the size of pilot's seat, etc, are easily gauged and extreme accuracy is less essential in this small scale. Cut off the nose and tail end and build up for the new streamlined nose and tail, as previously described for the 1:72 scale Lancastrian. Modify the rudders to the squarer type lower corners. Assemble the wings and inner Merlin nacelles carving away the top cowling of the outer nacelles that is moulded as part of the upper wing surfaces. Fill all the heavily engraved panel lines and sand smooth when dry.

For once I used wood to model the outer Nene cowlings—they were easily made from $\frac{3}{8}$ in dowel although having made one it would of course be a relatively simple matter to mould the two, in two halves each, from plastic card. The difficult bit may be carving away to make them appear 'hollow' but with a Precision Petite drill and a grinding bit this can be much simplified. An alternative is to use suitable plastic tube for the front $\frac{1}{8}$ in stuck on to the nose of the carved cowling and faired into the general shape. I did this for the tailpiece using parts cut from an Airfix Bloodhound missile. The central cones inside the cowling fronts were also cut from the same missile kit. When you have the general shape, carve away so that the cowling will fit up to the wing undersurface. The whole model can now be assembled, though a coat of gloss varnish on the wooden parts and on the Plastic Padding nose will help to seal these parts ready for painting.

The finish is overall silver with roundels as shown on the photograph.

Python test-bed

Another interesting Lancaster conversion is to the Python-Lancaster test-bed. Two Armstrong-Siddeley Python airscrew turbines were installed in place of the outer Merlins but with thrust lines some 22 inches below that of the original Merlins. Contra-rotating four bladed airscrews were fitted but, of course, full details have been given in the first part of this book.

Modification of the fuselage is similar to that described for a Lancastrian with the top turret position filled in, and nose and tail turret positions streamlined. I suggest that the tail turret could be cemented in place and filled with Plastic Padding or other body putty, but some formers will be necessary for the front position. All these are relatively simple modifications to be made to whichever kit you choose as a basis for your model.

The wings are assembled according to the kit instructions using only the inner nacelles, of course. The new Python nacelles are either carved from $\frac{3}{4}$ in dowel or

perhaps a refinement is to carve the rear only from dowel and make the parallel sided front part from Plastruct Tube. A check through your spares box is always worth while as you may find a plastic pill box, cigar tube or similar object that will do for this job. The contra-rotating four-bladed propeller assemblies will have to be built up either from scratch or using spinners and propeller blades from scrap kits. If you are lucky enough to have a couple of spare Frog Wyvern kits, or even Gannets, then you have a head start. Note the line of the flaps has to be altered to clear the tail pipe of the Python nacelles.

Avro York

The York was regarded by Avro as a stop-gap transport aircraft and, like a lot of similar makeshift types, it soldiered on for far longer than originally intended, in fact for 20 years or so. The tradition was started after World War 1 when the Vickers Vimy became the Vernon by the simple process of replacing the bomber fuselage with a fat cargo- or passenger-carrying body so that the Lancaster wings, engines and tail surfaces were wedded to a capacious and practical new fuselage to produce the useful York. Not the most beautiful of aircraft, the York nevertheless deserves a place in any collection of model aircraft if only for its association with the transport of many VIPs in the closing years of World War 2 and for its incomparable service during the Berlin airlift of 1948-49.

The conversion of a Lancaster to a York is, as you will have surmised, only a matter of producing an acceptable new fuselage to which to fasten the flying surfaces from any of the Lancaster kits you may prefer. The choice is yours but, if you want a model with flaps down, the Revell kit is to be preferred as this is marginally simpler. The Airfix kit will be acceptable if you want a straightforward wing. The latter has a slightly better undercarriage and was the one I chose in this instance. If you are feeling really ambitious then the Tamiya 1:48 scale kit would make a superb showpiece, especially with extra internal detail (a nice bit of extra research for you there). Bandai sell Jeeps to the same 1:48 scale if a large diorama loading them up through the wide side doors appeals to your sense of adventure.

There is, of course, a choice of construction methods, the first and perhaps the simplest is to go back to the Dark Ages when we carved from solid wood blocks and this gets

The completed model is a simple conversion of Novo's 1:96 scale kit.

Wooden dowel is used to carve the shape of the Nene test-bed cowlings.

my vote for a 1:144 scale or 1:96 scale model where the aim would be more to represent the overall outline and characteristics of the aircraft. In large 1:72 or 1:48 I think the absence of 'windows' would be too noticeable although they can be represented by punched discs cut from black transfer sheet and stuck in place after the model has been painted.

The fuselage is a nice box section and I see no reason why it cannot be built up using 60 thou plastic card for the top and bottom with at least 40 thou for the sides. A double thickness of 60 thou along top and bottom will ensure there is ample material at the corners to allow for filing and sanding to the required radius. By using this method at least you can open out the windows and glaze them behind with strips of clear plastic card. The nose and tail end can, of course, be built up using the method suggested for the Lancastrian or even, though the purists may shudder, by merely sticking a lump of Plasticine in place and moulding and shaping it to the correct contours. Never neglect the simple approach to your modelling problems—if done carefully this sort of solution will often get you out of trouble.

To build up the fuselage cut out, from 60 thou plastic card, a top and a bottom to the outline shown on the drawing (see rear endpaper). These are virtually the same except that the top will stop at the rear of the cockpit glazing and the bottom will need to be fractionally longer as it is slightly curved. Take it to the position in line with the front of the cockpit glazing, in other words ignoring the extreme nose section. You now need a further inside top and bottom, but cut 80 thou narrower, ie, to allow for the two 40 thou side pieces. Cement the inner and outer pieces together but hold them, by blocking them up on the bench, in a curve approximately to that of respectively the top and bottom lines of the fuselage.

Cut out two identical sides from 40 thou plastic card but undersize by 60 thou top and bottom, of course, to allow for the thickness of the parts that will overlap. Drill out all relevant 'windows' and score in the doors. I suggest if you are going in for open doors that they are well scored in but not removed until the fuselage is assembled. Do a test fit of the four basic parts, holding in place with Sellotape just as a check, then dismantle and cut out rectangular bulkheads for the nose just behind the

cockpit area, two for the wing fixing area, one behind the double doors and one at the rear.

Before assembly of the fuselage we must move to the wings as substantial spars will have to be made to hold them together. As the York fuselage is so much wider than the Lancaster, approximately 8 mm must be removed from the wing root. Note the fuselage does curve a little in plan view and it is therefore slightly less than this at the trailing edge. On the Airfix wing this is at the second row of rivets from the root. Cement the lower two wing halves together with substantial spars to bridge across the width of the fuselage. They will need careful setting up on the bench with the inboard sections flat and blocked up to give the correct dihedral angle at the tips. The spars should come to within 120 thou of the top surface, the idea being that they will adhere to the underside of the 'roof' of the fuselage. Cut out slots in the fuselage side pieces to accept these spars so that the wing will locate at the correct position and angle of incidence.

The sequence of assembly is now fairly critical. Glaze the inside of the 'windows' with clear plastic card in strips with gaps where the bulkheads will be, if not already done, and paint the interior to within, at the most, 60 thou of top and bottom. Assemble the interior bulkheads to the floor just at this stage, tacking them in place. Try not to get a bulkhead across a window! All this requires is careful marking out on the respective floor and sides. Cement the two sides to the floor/bulkheads and hold them with plenty of Sellotape. Paint the floor and all sides of the bulkheads. Paint the wing spar where it goes inside the fuselage, also the inside of the top. If you are detailing the interior now is the time—after the next stage it will be too late.

Slip the lower wing assembly with the joining spars into the slots in the fuselage sides. If all goes well the root 'rib' will fit snug up to the sides. The last stage is to cement the top in place, in fact it is a good idea just to slip it in place while the sides-to-floor unit dries and then take it off again to fit in the wing. The upper wing halves will require trimming at the root and then they can also be cemented into place to the lower halves and will, with luck, lie with their top surfaces in line with the top of the fuselage. When the whole issue is dry then the fuselage 'corners' have to be filed off and sanded to the 'round' edge as shown on the cross sections. It may in fact be an idea to file these corners roughly to shape to some extent before the fuselage parts are cemented together but of course this must only be partly done. I also found it useful to mask the 'windows' with Humbrol Maskol before doing a lot of sanding as it does prevent a build up of dust and debris on the window glazing.

That is one of the ways of making a York fuselage, the rest of the model merely requires the addition of the nacelles, undercarriage and tail unit from the kit. No, I had not forgotten the central fin, that comes from a spare Lancaster or if your scrap box has not got one, a bit of plastic card, and you will have to mould a cockpit canopy from clear plastic card.

Just one small point: some of the Yorks had modified rudders as described for the Lancastrian and it is difficult

Shaping the two halves of a Contrail York fuselage on a sheet of wet-and-dry taped down to an offcut of hardboard.

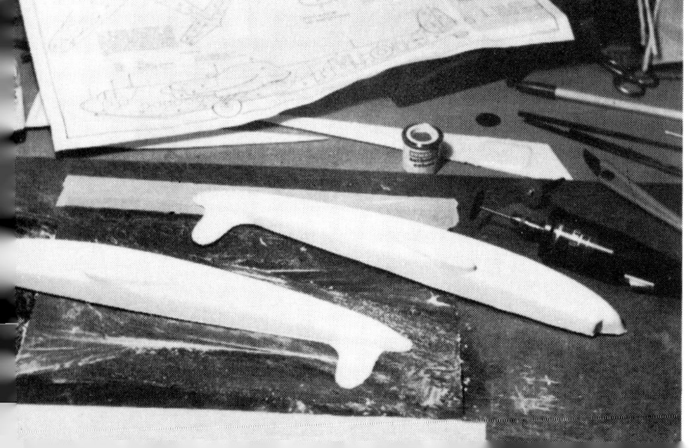

Airfix wings and tail surfaces attached to the Contrail York fuselage with masked glazing and undercoat applied to the fuselage.

A York fuselage assembled and the lower wing halves joined with scrap plastic spars.

to paint the inner nacelles.

If you do not fancy any of the methods so far described then try a Contrail Vac-form conversion kit which is, I think, still available from the indefatigable Gordon Sutcliffe. This consists of the fuselage, which is in two halves, and the internal bulkheads all on the one sheet of substantial plastic, and a moulded cockpit. This is one of Gordon's early kits and I know he will not mind me saying it is not quite up to the standard of some of the latest. In fact, he may by now have re-done it but nevertheless I did think it a bit short and injected a section in the middle. You will see from my photographs that I cut out the wing section from the sides to enable the complete wing to pass through. Gordon's suggestion was to let in wing spars and, in fact, this method could be used for the scratch-built fuselage instead of my method of dropping in the complete wing lower surfaces.

My object was to ensure a good strong wing which would not sag when the full weight of the model was on the undercarriage.

Whichever method of construction you use there are many effective colour schemes, mostly natural metal finish, from which you can choose. They were, apart from RAF versions, used by BOAC, Skyways, Hunting Clan, Air Charter, British Southern American Airways, Dan-Air, Eagle, French Aeronavale and many others around the world. The use of a Metalskin finish would be particularly appropriate and effective on a York, though I would imagine cutting out the 'port holes' to be rather tedious.

Finally there is always LV626, the first York prototype which was converted to C II configuration with Bristol Hercules VI radial engines, yellow undersides and a brown/green camouflage. That really is a conversion to ponder!

The finished model, hand painted and embellished with transfers from the spares box.

Chapter Twelve

Lancaster in detail

The largest scale kit of the Lancaster is that in 1:48 scale produced by Tamiya and perhaps, naturally, this is the one for the super-detailing fanatic. This is available in B1/BIII versions or as Grand Slam/Dam Buster variants and the following suggestions for detailing will apply mainly to both kits although some features will be related to only the B1/BIII.

A decision will have to be made before you start your model as to the amount of detail you wish to incorporate —you may want to go further than I did or just to make one or two alterations to the basic model. You may even think the kit is good enough as it stands and, of course, it is a very good kit in all respects but the manufacturer, as does the individual modeller, has to draw the line somewhere.

To incorporate additional detailing means diverging from the instruction sheet sequence of construction as it is vital to cut away parts required before adding the substructures.

We will therefore start with the main fuselage halves by removing the entrance door on the starboard side. Aircraft undergoing maintenance invariably had the door open, in fact photographs suggest that it is seldom closed when on the ground unless parked at dispersal.

There were usually some jobs being done between missions and ground crew would be busy inside and outside the aircraft resupplying ammunition and checking the instrumentation, etc. The door position is well marked on the outside and can be cut out completely with a mini circular saw or the point of a razor saw. After this is cut away, fix all the glazing strips in place. The inside of the port side is, of course, visible now the door has been opened out and must therefore be detailed to represent the fuselage formers and stringers similar to those on the kit in the cockpit area.

I used 0.5 × 0.5 mm Riko ministrip, first cementing stringers in place to coincide with the lines of rivets on the outside skin. The formers were then cemented over these, curving to fit the inside curves of the fuselage, also using the external riveting as a guide. In addition, at the rear of the fuselage, there are some bracing struts between the rear turret ring and the rear of the tailplane spar, and the ring and the fuselage bottom. A floor has to be fitted inside the two fuselage halves and to do this requires a bit of trial and error to get the correct taper. Just inside the door is a step to bridge the ammunition chutes which feed the rear turret position. The Elsan toilet to the rear of the door can be made from $\frac{1}{4}$ in thick round sprue and cemented central to the floor. It also serves as a step to the tailplane spar.

The next point to consider is the bomb bay (applicable to B1/BII version), as it is obvious that if you are depicting the aircraft undergoing maintenance it would not have a bomb load aboard. It is also fairly safe to say that the bomb doors would be open as they opened due to falling pressure in the system. The hydraulic supply is via engine-driven pumps on both inner engines with an emergency hand pump mounted on the port side of the fuselage between the armoured bulkhead and the front spar. The bomb bay in the kit unfortunately has large locating stubs on which to attach the bombs and therefore to depict an empty bomb bay you must remove these. I found a pair of nail clippers useful to nibble away the majority of these stubs and the rest is a matter of patient carving away with a craft knife. The detail can be re-instated using stretched sprue. The crutching or steadies for the 4,000 lb bomb can

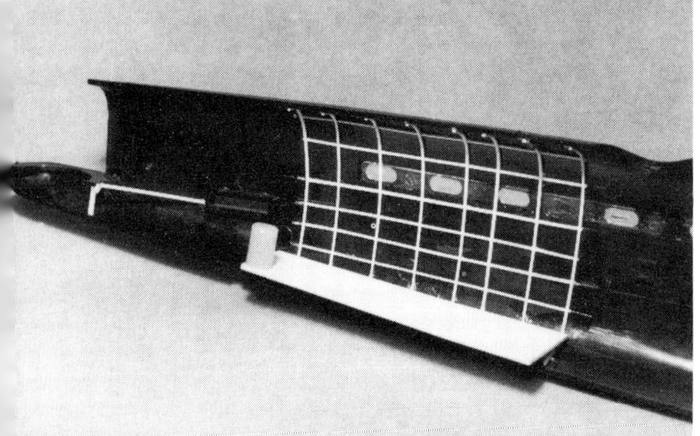

Fuselage formers and stringers built up inside the port fuselage side. The floor and Elsan have been added.

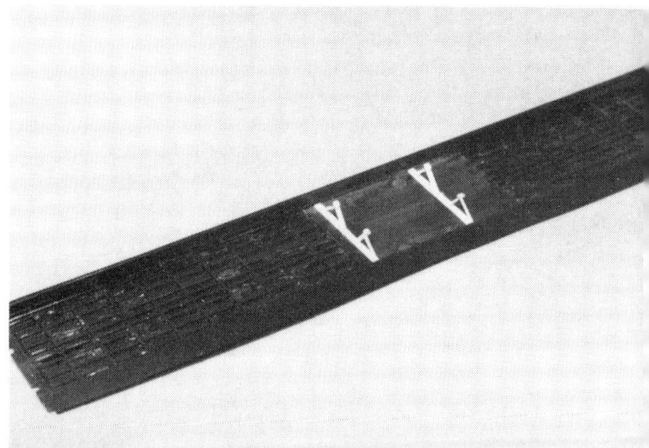

The bomb attachment stubs have been removed and steadies added to the mid section.

be made up from Microstrip, plastic rod and stretched sprue as shown in the photographs, using the kit bomb as a guide for dimensions. Do not fit these at this stage as they will be very prone to damage.

Fuselage interior

Tamiya have very generously fitted out the interior of the cockpit and you may even consider there is quite sufficient for your model—in any case it is difficult to see all of that provided when the model is complete. However, there are just a few points that may be worth modifying. It is strange that there are only three throttles on the console but that is hardly worth taking a lot of trouble over and the dashboard controls generally are very well done and the transfers for the various panels help to give life to this area. The pilot's seat mounting is very much simplified, it should be a tubular frame but again it is barely visible when the model is finished. The navigator's chair should pivot on a frame from one of the tubular posts (part B32) and I made this up from plastic rod. An Anglepoise-type lamp for the navigator's bench, possibly some thin paper charts, are also possibilities for the table. To the right of the pilot's seat (which incidentally can be modelled with arm rests up or down) is situated a trimming tab control which comprised a large elevator trim tab handwheel, a rudder trim tab control handwheel on top and aileron trim tab handwheel on the front. The flaps' control lever is also mounted to this assembly which consists of a conical pedestal with a basically rectangular gearbox and bearing support for the various handwheels. These are all modelled from scrap sprue and card with the various handwheels from punched plastic card discs; details should be fairly obvious from the photographs. A length of plastic rod should also be used for the rather prominent pilot's seat adjusting lever which is on the left side of the seat. Careful painting of the interior in Aircraft Grey-Green (Humbrol HD 1) with detail picked out in matt black with a touch of white round any of the instruments is about all that it is sensible to do in this scale.

A couple of modifications should be made to the starboard side of the fuselage interior to the flight engineer's seat (parts B17 and B10) which you will see is too long—it would foul the trim tab controls if left as in the kit. Cut this across to leave a seat that protrudes 10 mm and cement direct to the fuselage side. Shorten the support bracket to fit. Also I am sure there should be a handrail to help access to the bomb aimer's position. This is modelled as in the Lancaster at RAF Scampton, Lincoln, but a drawing in *Aeroplane* of 1942 vintage shows a ladder in this position. You may also like to cut out a 'couch' for the bomb aimer's position which can be fitted through the nose when the two halves of the fuselage have been cemented together. The size of this couch can be judged from the doors engraved underneath the nose of the kit parts. A seat cushion should also be fitted in front and rear turrets. The rear turret has two sliding doors and the position of this aperture is certainly engraved on part F8. By carefully cutting this out you will be able to see, though not very clearly, through the full

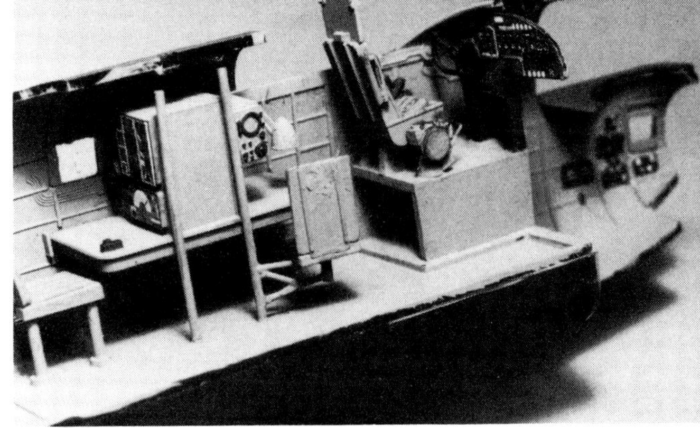

Above *The port side interior showing the modified navigator's seat and pilot's trim controls. Note the navigator's lamp and the trim tab controls.*

Below *The view down into the bomb aimer's position in the Gate Guardian at Scampton.*

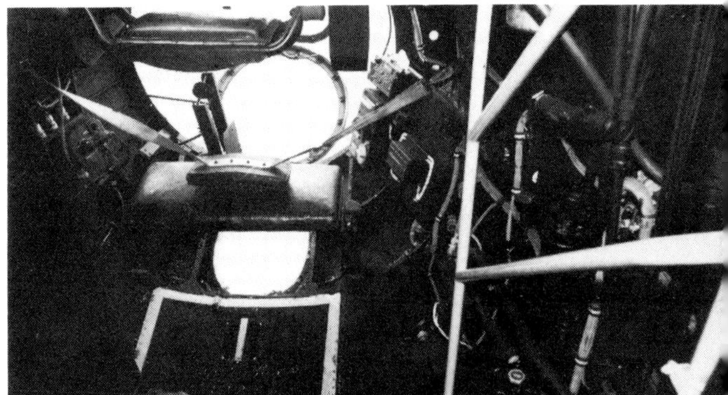

Above *The rear turret interior of the Scampton Lancaster.*

Below *Note the sliding access doors with 'port hole' windows to the rear turret. Only the left door is shut in this shot.*

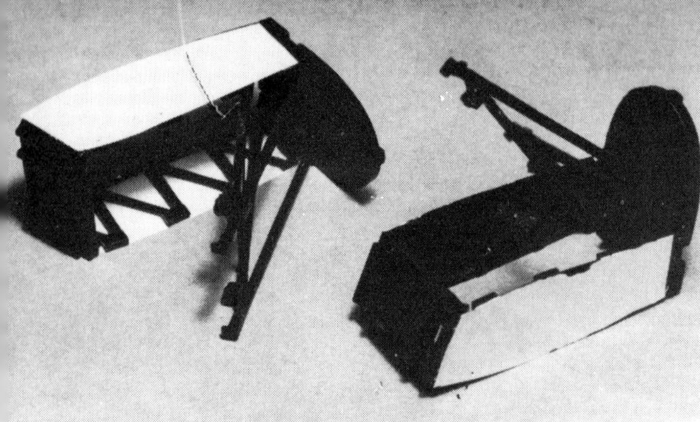

length of the fuselage. The doors each have a round port hole window and they slide inside the turret.

Wing sections

We can leave the fuselage for the moment and move on to the undercarriage assemblies which are quite tricky to assemble but very substantial when finished. Not quite correct are the open ribs of the undercarriage well sides (parts A30 and A31) and these should be sheeted in with 5 thou plastic card on the outside of the sub-assembly. They will still slip through the aperture in the lower surface of the wing so there will be no problems there. Remember also, at a later stage, to fit short lengths of plastic rod from the undercarriage leg stays to the wheel doors (parts A12 and A15). The doors are pulled in automatically as the legs retract—there are no separate jacks. I also filed a flat on each tyre so that it appeared to be taking the weight of the aircraft.

The Tamiya kit is fortunately free of 'moving' gimmicks but if you wish to set the ailerons to a different position it is simple to cut them away from the main wing and re-cement as required. More complicated is the re-location of the flaps but I think that an aircraft displayed 'on the ground' should have its flaps down. The first move is to cut the flaps away from the lower wing half and clean up the parts with a file. The tubular spar is now added to the inner side and the trailing edge detailed with 10 thou plastic card with lightening holes drilled as shown in the photograph. The position of the ribs is gauged by reference to the engraved detail on the outer surface and these were added from 0.5 mm square mini strip. The end ribs are filled in with 10 thou plastic card.

The rear spar has now to be built up to the inside of the lower wing half and this is made from a $\frac{1}{4}$ in wide strip of 15 thou plastic card. Sellotape the two parts of the wing together while this spar is cemented in place. Split the wings apart when dry and trim the spar to a good fit, if required. Paint the inside of the wheel well and then you can finally cement the wings together. The underside of the wing can then be fitted with rib detail and trailing edge as we did for the flaps.

Engine nacelles

Study of the inboard nacelles will show that the rear part overlaps the flaps and, in fact, this goes inside the forward nacelle when the flaps are down. The first stage is therefore to cut it off along the engraved line and as the thickness of the plastic is too great to allow it to slip inside, cut a wedge-shaped section from the cut off end to correspond to the angle of flap that you have decided upon. Both inner nacelle ends must be identical to ensure that port and starboard flap angles are the same but leave assembly to the wings until after the nacelles are complete.

The kit provides only two engines and it is immaterial which you do, if any. I opted for the two starboard engines and, as you will see, I took the outer a stage further by removing the lower cowling parts. You could go even further and ignore the nacelle cowlings and fairings and just build up the frame and engine bearers.

The kit engine bearers are a bit basic and can be improved by adding the diagonal struts from plastic rod. I found it simpler to build up the basic engine, leaving off the exhausts (parts A36) and the camshaft covers (parts A24) mounting this in the modified bearers and to the bulkhead (E8 or E9) and setting this up without cementing in the port nacelle. This ensures that the propeller shaft will come in the correct position when all is dry. Assuming that you are to remove the lower cowlings then you will not use the radiator (part A19) but will substitute a 15 thou plastic card disc cut the same size as the spinner. This cements over the propeller shaft and supports the cowling framework which is from 0.5 mm square Ministrip. The camshaft covers do not give the engine the characteristic Merlin look, they are distinctly tapering to the front and this illusion can be created by packing up at the rear with scrap 20 thou plastic card. Fill any gaps underneath with body putty and also re-shape the rear ends with a bit of putty, again as shown on the photographs. A good look at a Merlin engine in one of the many museums will help here. Alternatively, if you have made any of the 1:24 scale Airfix kits, Spitfire, Hurricane or Mustang, or have the previous books in this series, then you will have a very good idea of what the top half of a Merlin should look like. The exhaust stubs in the Tamiya kit are not too good either. Of course, there are limitations to what can be moulded in this scale and I suggest that at least the heat shield behind the stubs should be thinned down or replaced with thin plastic card sheet. Photographs show that they were trough-shaped and these can be built up using 10 thou plastic card for the base, square ended at the front and rounded at the rear. The sides are added with very thin Microstrip and the stubs, cut from those in the kit, cemented in place individually.

The radiator underneath the engine can be built up using the kit part A38 for the front and adding a box from 30 thou plastic card behind this, filed to shape and with the straps added from Microstrip. Cement it in place underneath the engine sump and add the pipework from plastic rod. The location of the pipework has to be gauged by reference to photographs but I think the main thing is to aim for the general effect and try to represent the main pipes as well as possible. If you have seen an actual Merlin installed then you will know that the engine pipework and wiring is very complicated and to reproduce it accurately in 1:48 scale virtually impossible. Look through photographs and try for this general impression on your model, using plastic rod and various thicknesses of stretched sprue but do not try to cram too much in and spoil the effect.

Assemble the completed engines and nacelles to the wings, both port and starboard as you have decided, and paint all the engine parts matt black with perhaps just a slight sheen, or add this with dilute varnish after the matt paint is dry. The cowling supports are grey/green. I would suggest that the undersurface of the wings also be painted before the wings are joined to the fuselage.

The flaps and inner nacelle fairings should be cemented to the wing and the actuating rods added from thin plastic rod. Also the other small detail parts, aileron controls,

Above *The flaps cut away from a Tamiya Lancaster.*

Below *Starboard flaps are built up on the 'inside' with Microstrip.*

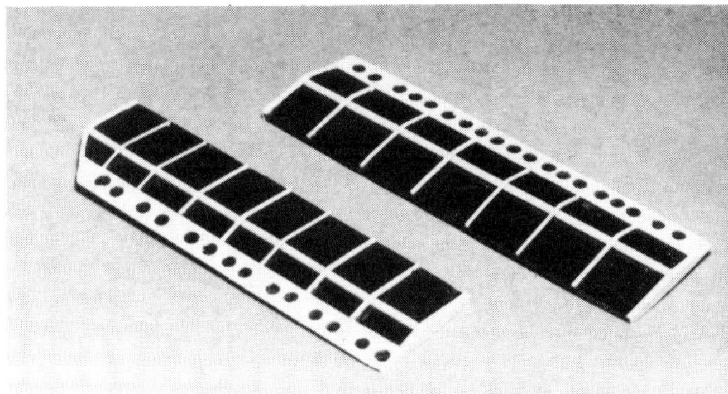

Above *Spars and strengthening gussets to the lower wing halves.*

Below *The finished flaps assembled to the model.*

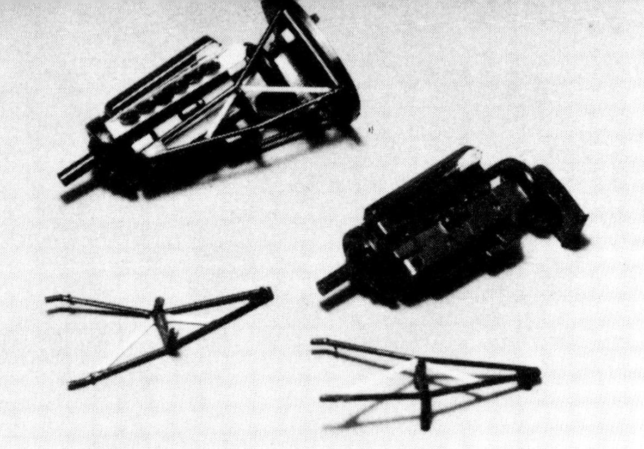

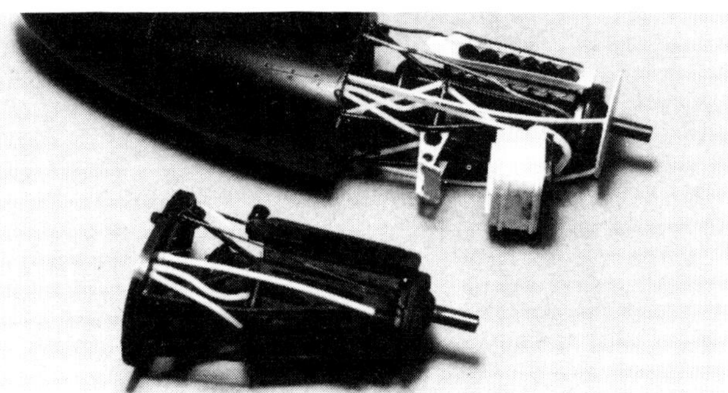

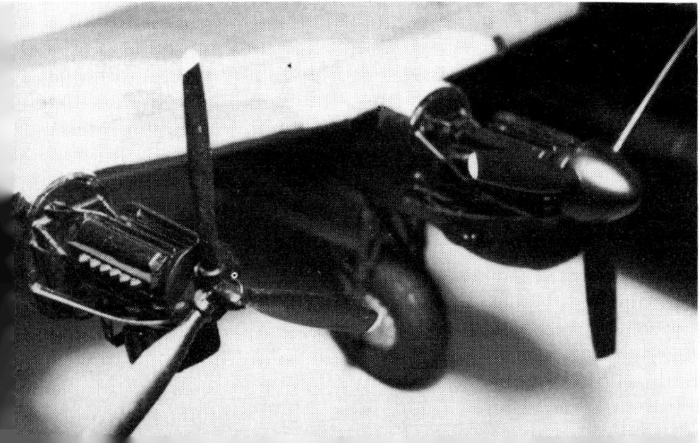

etc, as supplied in the kit, can be added.

My model is left with detachable wings and if you are short of storage or permanent display space then you may find this a good idea. The design and fit of the wings are so good that the model will stand perfectly in this state. To ensure the camouflage scheme is accurate the wings will have to be slipped into place temporarily to mark the pattern where the wing joins the fuselage.

Fuselage assembly

To return to the fuselage, if you have finished off all the interior that you consider adequate, have a final check to be absolutely sure that all painting has been done and after a trial run cement the two halves together. Again Tamiya design allows for the turrets to be fitted after both halves are cemented together which certainly simplifies construction. Painting the turret frames is perhaps the most tedious job on the model and I can only recommend patience and a steady hand. I would suggest also that turrets are not fitted in place until after the fuselage has been painted.

Having joined the fuselage and filled and sanded away any join lines that show, the next stage must be fitting the bomb bay doors. These are a bit tricky and I had just to trim the ends of the front and rear jacks (parts G10 and G11) to get the doors to lie true.

If you are fitting the radar blister do not forget to paint the underside of the fuselage, inside the blister, before cementing this in place. Also paint the fuselage top inside the rear of the cockpit canopy before fitting the canopy in place.

The fairing for the top turret and the top 'window', the aerials and pitot tube, etc, can also be fitted now. I also built up the tubular support frames for the bomb site in the nose and fitted the floor glazing, painting the frame of this after it is in place.

The fuselage undersurface can be painted at this stage, before the tailplane is cemented in place. Note that most of the fuselage side windows are painted over, only those at the front are left clear as shown on the box artwork. The photograph of the completed model on the instruction sheet is surely not correct for a machine of this period.

I painted fuselage, wing and tailplane undersurfaces at this stage and my first coat of Matt Black (Humbrol 33) did not in fact look right so I decided a second coat was indicated, and as usual I had nearly run out. My local model shop was out of stock of Black 33 and the nearest alternative was Coal Black (Humbrol 85) and this I find gives a super finish with just a slight sheen, it looks to me just right for a model in this scale. All the inside surfaces like the undercarriage doors and inside the flaps were left in Matt 33 to give a contrast in surface finish.

The airscrews can also be painted in the same Coal Black together with spinners, of course, but I would suggest they are best fitted last of all as they always seem to get in the way while painting. You will notice that I have left off the spinner from the starboard outer and to do this you must modify the hub. This is done by carving away the 'disc' at the centre and cementing a boss on the front. Careful with the carving as there is not a lot holding the blades together at the centre. The boss is a stub of sprue with rounded nose, drilled to take a short length of thin plastic rod. This thin rod is also used to make the rings round the blade roots.

The rest of the model is just the final painting of the camouflage scheme and application of the transfers for your chosen aircraft with perhaps a few modifications to the cockpit canopy. My model was almost complete when I heard of a cockpit canopy which had been found by Mike Hodgson of the Lincolnshire Aviation Society. Now, it is not often that it is possible to see a Lancaster canopy close to and, though slightly ravaged by time, this did answer one or two questions that I had formerly been unable to resolve. As mentioned in the chapter on Painting and Display, the two horizontal frame members are inside the perspex but what I had been unable to verify was that some of the hoop frames are also on the inside. The cockpit is perhaps the focal point of the model and it is important therefore to try to get this area right. Part of the frame, from the windscreen back to the rear edge of the rectangular side windows, is of tubular construction on the inside with capping strips on the outside, the perspex being sandwiched between and held together with countersunk bolts and nuts. The rear is framed partly like this and partly has a tubular frame with bolts, not rivets, countersunk into the perspex, with some framing in wood held with countersunk screws. The inside frame is painted matt black, with any outer frame matching the camouflage colour. The only way I can suggest to reproduce this is to construct a framework—to go inside the transparent canopy. To protect the inside of the canopy paint it with a coat of Humbrol Maskol and either build direct inside or as an alternative, use Plasticine to make a mould. This must be worked until it is very soft to go inside the canopy without damaging or distorting it. Allow it to harden and carefully remove it, then gouge out the lines of the framework and build up the frame around the Plasticine using Microstrip and thin rod. When dry the frame can be removed from the Plasticine and should, with luck, fit inside the canopy. Of course, it should all be painted before finally assembling in position. The outer frame can be added with painted Sellotape strip, painted on direct or you could make strips of transfers by overpainting old transfer sheet with the camouflage colour. If you assemble the frame inside the canopy itself then again, of course, when dry remove it to paint before re-assembling in position. An alternative to protecting with Maskol is to use strips of Sellotape inside the canopy but take care when removing them.

This may seem an awful lot of trouble but I do think it is worth taking a bit of care over this, the most important point of the model. It really is the bit that most admirers of your handywork will be peering through to see what is inside. I hope they will be impressed with the effort that you have put in and with the skill of the Tamiya craftsmen responsible for the kit, one of the very best bomber kits available to date, and one which is a real pleasure to build.

Above and below *Two views of the cockpit canopy which show the framework in some detail.*

Above *A framework built up to go inside the clear canopy. Here it is shown unpainted.*

Below *The framework has been painted black and installed inside the canopy and the outer frame painted on the outside.*

Chapter Thirteen

Painting and display

The trend for modellers today is to spend more time and effort in the realistic display of their models, and I hope in this chapter to discuss a few ideas for realistic settings.

Of course, the final finish of your model was settled before you started construction and the quality of that finish was decided by the construction. Neat, clean construction is vital and slipshod workmanship cannot be disguised by a coat of paint. Not all kits fit together perfectly and filling of cracks will be almost inevitable. My own favourite filler is Squadron Green Putty but this is poisonous, inflammable and you may be allergic to its fumes, so do be extremely careful and keep it well away from younger members of the family, the cat or your pet budgie. It does finish well and can be filed and sanded (with wet-and-dry) so as to be virtually undetectable under a coat of paint. For the larger filling jobs, as mentioned in earlier chapters, I have found that Plastic Padding is ideal though a coat of varnish to seal its slight porosity is advisable. The main requirements of a good filler are that it should not shrink as it dries, it must be capable of being filed and sanded, and it must take a good finish.

Careful construction and filling any gaps are therefore the first steps to a good paint finish. The worst stumbling block before you even get out your paints and brushes is dust. Get rid of it, brush it out of the panel lines, blow it off, wipe with a damp cloth then do it all again. Take your model outside to do all this if possible—at least it gets the dust out of the place instead of leaving it floating in the air, ready to settle on your wet paint. Finger marks are as bad as dust, so keep your hands clean and free from perspiration all the time. Try Swarfega before you wash your hands—it takes some of the grease out of your skin. Just a quick tip—if you have had to do some heavy sanding to get rid of, say, a joint line, a quick brush over with Mek-Pak will restore the gloss finish of the surface. Try it on scrap parts first as you may find your brush sticks to the model if you are not quick enough.

We are just about ready to paint, you think? Nowhere near, the next vital step is to stir the paint. Do not spoil your efforts by using old tins of half dried up paint—invest in a new tin or so from time to time. My own procedure for mixing my paints is first to shake the tin and then to open it up and stir it with a piece of split cane to ensure that there is no sediment sticking to the bottom. I do this for all the colours I am going to use on the model and then, replacing all the lids, I wrap the tins in my paint rag and shake them forever—at least it seems forever—checking with a stir regularly and then further shaking. If

you have a Mini-drill then a wire stirrer could be made to take out a little of the wrist ache. I must stress that it really is vital to make absolutely sure the paint is well and truly mixed no matter what brand of paint you are using. Once you have them all mixed it is relatively easy to keep them that way by a further shake-up at each modelling session.

Good brushes are your next requirement and a five pence brush from your local chain store just will not do for this job. I know they are expensive but artists' quality sable is a good buy and will last for years if carefully cleaned and washed immediately after use.

Of course, actually applying the paint is a matter of practice but with properly prepared paint and a good brush you are nearly there. For larger areas you want a decent sized brush, say a number three or at least a two. Silver seems to be a problem to some modellers and for this on, say, the Lancastrian, I used a long-haired number two sable and did not have a lot of trouble. Make all final strokes in the direction of the line of flight, that is, nose to tail on the fuselage, and leading edge to trailing edge on the wings and tail surfaces. Any slight streaking will then look perfectly natural on the finished model.

Camouflage colours should be no particular problem but always try to do the lightest colour first then mistakes can be corrected when the darker shade is applied. I always draw the demarcation lines in soft pencil as a guide for the first colour and then carefully paint up to this line with the second.

A steady hand is required for the glazing bars on some kits particularly as these are not defined too clearly. Some of my models had these frames applied with pre-painted Sellotape which is quite useful but not particularly easy to do with silver paint. I think the trick is to stick a length of Sellotape to a tin lid, paint it in the required colour and use it as soon as it is dry. If left for several days before use the paint can get too brittle and as soon as the strips are cut it will flake off. I found this method particularly useful for the 1:96 scale Novo Lancaster which really required a fine line. Note that the horizontal frame from a point behind the step up, ie, behind the rectangular side windows, is inside the clear moulding as are some of the hoops. These should be painted on the inside and if you feel up to it, rivets could be painted on the outside though, to be practical, this would really only apply to the Tamiya models.

Transfers in some kits still pose the problem of the glue squeezing out when they are pressed into place. It is essential to remove any air or water bubbles by gently smoothing the transfers with a soft cloth. The only answer where this occurs is to go over it and touch up with paint. Of course, you will cut out the individual parts from the transfer sheet as close to the edge of the colour as possible, as an unsightly shiny edge to the markings spoils many an otherwise well-finished model, so watch this point. Where it is not possible to cut away the edges touch them up with camouflage colour.

Weathering, as it is commonly called, is not a way to disguise a poor paint job but can, if used with discretion, be an aid to a realistic effect, especially where the model is to be displayed in a diorama.

The way in which you eventually display your particular model will depend on the space you have available and, of course, your whole reason for making it in the first place. I model as a relaxation from the daily grind, because I like making things and, to be honest, it matters not a lot what it is, aircraft, tanks, cars—anything. But each model presents some sort of challenge, a lot of research and some problems, and unfortunately at the moment I have a very limited space for display. I suspect this is typical but a lot of modellers specialise more in one particular field which is, perhaps, a pity as the dyed-in-the-wool aircraft modeller can miss out on other aspects like railway vehicles, figures and scenic modelling.

The bomber, in this case we are discussing the Lancaster, lends itself particularly well to a diorama scene as this type of aircraft always seems to be surrounded by a host of supply vehicles and ground crew (see page 96). The present kit market now provides plenty of these auxiliaries and first to come to mind must be the Airfix range of RAF vehicle sets. My own book in the *Airfix Magazine Guide* series *Modelling RAF Vehicles* was written to help modellers extend the Airfix series and contains drawings for many vehicles suitable for display with your Lancaster including crewbuses, refuellers, transporters, utilities, ambulances, vans, general service trucks, workshop trucks, cranes, etc.

The Airfix groundcrew figure sets and the tractor and bomb trailers in the Short Stirling kit are also certainly useful and the 1:72 scale metal figures from New Hope Design, Rothbury, Northumberland can also be used to add that extra touch of realism.

The standard Lancaster bomber model can therefore be displayed with an endless variety of other figures and vehicles and, of course, the best references are photographs of the aircraft in service, some of which are to be found in this book. An alternative is to model a preserved Lancaster and re-create its present surroundings, for example, NX611 the gate guardian at RAF Scampton, near Lincoln. This is displayed with the Dam Buster bomb and a pair of 2,200 lb Grand Slam bombs. PA474, KM-B of the Battle of Britain Flight, could be displayed alongside its fellow Hurricane and Spitfire in an 'at home' setting with crowds of civilians gazing with the awe and admiration it so well deserves. Civilian figures are available from many model railway stockists and this type of display would, I think, be a little more unusual and colourful than a wartime scene.

The Revell Dam Buster Lancaster offers scope for a particularly interesting display and one that I think is not commonly considered. To load the 'bomb' the fairing in front of the bomb (part 54 in the kit) was hinged open in similar fashion to the bomb doors of a normal Lancaster. The belt drive is removed before the doors are opened and the eyebolt fitted in the fuselage is now some 17 ft 6 in from ground level and the clearance for the bomb is of the tailplane. The tail is now lifted by a Coles 10-ton Crane (the Airfix kit would be suitable for this) to allow the bomb on a Type E bomb trolley to be pulled (tractor from the Stirling kit) into place from the rear. The top of the eyebolt fitted in the fuselage is now some 17 feet 6 in from ground level and the clearance for the bomb is about 3 in under the fuselage—a pretty tight fit. Two loading slings round the bomb are used, with hoists fitted inside the aircraft, to lift the bomb the few inches off its cradle on the bomb trolley to the fittings under the aircraft. The trolley is pulled away and the aircraft tail lowered gently to the ground, the eyebolt removed and replaced with a rubber cap, the fairing closed up and the drive belt re-fitted. This whole sequence presents, with attendant groundcrew, interesting display possibilities but would require some support to be provided, say by incorporating a wire 'gallows' in the crane vehicle.

The Air Sea Rescue Lancaster has already been discussed and its display on a fine wire support over a 'sea' in which a ditched aircraft and crew in life jackets or rubber boat are floating would, I think, make a very impressive yet simple set-piece.

The 'civil versions of Lancastrian and York lend themselves to a more peaceful and colourful setting with civilian passengers boarding and airport service vehicles in attendance. These aircraft, in particular the York, were used for the Berlin airlift and extremely busy scenes of either loading or unloading with mixed civilian and military vehicles and personnel are possible. There are plenty of 1:72 scale Jeeps and a scene loading these through the side door of the York is another interesting possibility.

These suggestions are all for display of a complete aircraft but for one particular incident of R5845 (a Mk 1, coded YW-T which crashed in Lincolnshire). The recovery of this aircraft on a convoy of Queen Marys with motor cycle escort would make a fascinating exercise in modelling techniques. The additional detail of wing ribs, fuselage joints and internal detail, scratchbuilt engines (though maybe not strictly necessary as they would be covered with tarpaulins) recovery cranes, trolleys, jacks, the Queen Marys with Bedford and Commer tractor units, crash damage to the aircraft, fitters, drivers, the whole cavalcade could all be included. A fascinating thought and for me it is a 'one of these days' idea but that, or a similar situation, I leave as a thought to add to the many you must already have from the pictures, drawings and colour schemes we have included in this book. That is all I have room for except to say I hope you may have found a few useful ideas and that you too have enjoyed modelling the Lancaster from one or more of the kits available. I should like to thank the kit manufacturers and wish you 'happy modelling'.

R5845 of 1660 HCU Swinderby crashed at Windthorpe near Newark in October 1943 and is here being taken away for repairs. It flew again from Langar on January 19 1944. Such a scene is ideal for presentation as a diorama.

Bibliography

Avro Aircraft since 1908 A.J. Jackson, Putnam 1974.

Avro Lancaster I Garbett & Goulding, Profile No 65.

Avro Lancaster II Bruce Robertson, Profile No 235.

Avro Lancaster B I/III Francis K. Mason, Major Archive.

Avro Lancaster in Unit Service Garbett & Goulding, Aircam No 12 1971.

Avro Manchester Chaz Bowyer, Profile No 260

Avro York Donald Hannah, Profile No 168.

Bomber County T.N. Hancock, Lincs Library Service 1978.

Bomber Squadrons of the RAF & their Aircraft P.J.R. Moyes, Macdonald 1971.

Lancaster—the Story of a Famous Bomber Bruce Robertson, Harleyford 1964.

Lancaster at War Garbett & Goulding, Ian Allan 1971.

Lancaster Manual RAF Museum, Arms & Armour Press 1977.

Lincolnshire Air War Sid Finn, Control Column Publications 1973.

RCAF Squadrons and Aircraft Kostenuk & Griffin, National Museums of Canada 1977.

Story of a Lanc Goulding, Garbett & Partridge, RAF Scampton 1974.

Very Special Lancaster F.E. Dymond, RAF Museum.

Veteran and Vintage Aircraft, 4th edition Leslie Hunt, Garnstone Press 1974.

White Rose Base Brian Rapier, Control Column Publications 1972.

44 (Rhodesia) Squadron, RAF, on operations Alan N. White, 1977.

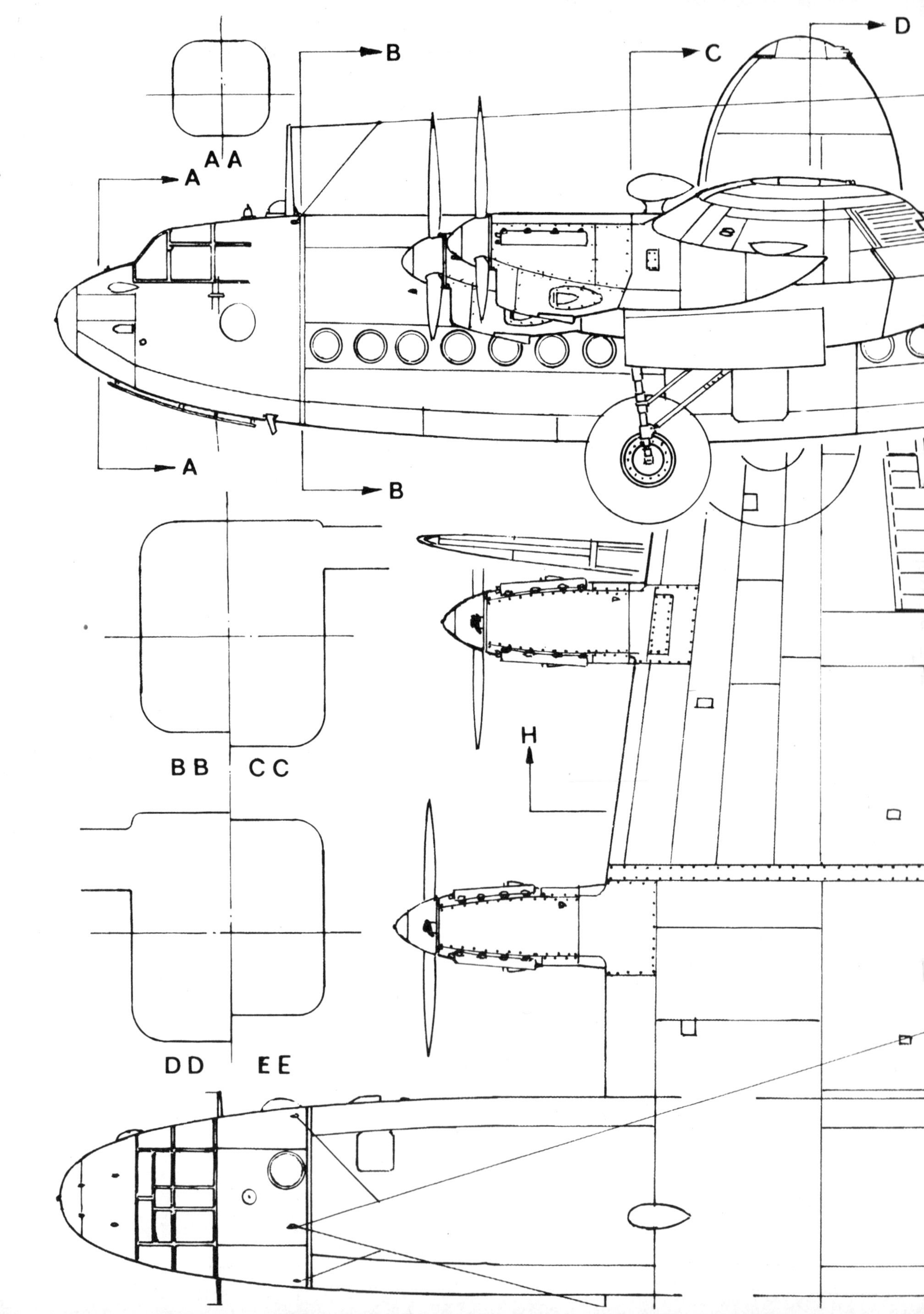
A A A
A
B
A
A
B B C C
D D E E
B
C
D
H